Survival Guide for Beginners 2020 And The Beginner's Vegetable Garden 2020

The Complete Beginner's Guide to Gardening and Survival in 2020

Leslie Martin

© Copyright 2020 by Leslie Martin. All right reserved.

The work contained herein has been produced with the intent to provide relevant knowledge and information on the topic on the topic described in the title for entertainment purposes only. While the author has gone to every extent to furnish up to date and true information, no claims can be made as to its accuracy or validity as the author has made no claims to be an expert on this topic. Notwithstanding, the reader is asked to do their own research and consult any subject matter experts they deem necessary to ensure the quality and accuracy of the material presented herein.

This statement is legally binding as deemed by the Committee of Publishers Association and the American Bar Association for the territory of the United States. Other jurisdictions may apply their own legal statutes. Any reproduction, transmission or copying of this material contained in this work without the express written consent of the copyright holder shall be deemed as a copyright violation as per the current legislation in force on the date of publishing and subsequent time thereafter. All additional works derived from this material may be claimed by the holder of this copyright.

The data, depictions, events, descriptions and all other information forthwith are considered to be true, fair and accurate unless the work is expressly described as a work of fiction. Regardless of the nature of this work, the Publisher is exempt from any responsibility of actions taken by the reader in conjunction with this work. The Publisher acknowledges that the reader acts of their own accord and releases the author and Publisher of any responsibility for the observance of tips, advice, counsel, strategies and techniques that may be offered in this volume.

TABLE OF CONTENTS

Survival Guide for Beginners 2020

INTRODUCTION 1

CHAPTER 1 *Essential Task List Of Survival* 3

    MINOR EMERGENCY SURVIVAL TASK LIST 4

    MAJOR EMERGENCY SURVIVAL TASK LIST 10

CHAPTER 2 *On-Grid Survival Guide* 15

    SHORT-TERM VS. LONG-TERM ON-GRID SURVIVAL 16

    SECURING SAFETY 17

    SECURING WATER 18

    SECURING FOOD 19

    SECURING FIRE 20

    SECURING SHELTER 21

CHAPTER 3 *Off-Grid Survival Guide* 22

    THE PREPARATION BEFORE THE EMERGENCY 23

    SECURING YOUR FIVE NEEDS FOR SURVIVAL 24

    SETTING YOUR SHORT-TERM SURVIVAL EXPECTATIONS 25

    SETTING YOUR LONG-TERM SURVIVAL EXPECTATIONS 25

CHAPTER 4 *Necessary Survival Materials* 27

    TOOLS FOR WATER 28

    TOOLS FOR SHELTER 28

    TOOLS FOR FIRE 29

    TOOLS FOR FOOD 30

    TOOLS FOR SAFETY 31

Tools for Travel 32

CHAPTER 5 *The First Essential: Water* **34**

    Locating and Accessing Water..35

    Purifying and Storing Water..37

    Building Your Camp Near a Body of Water..38

    Securing Long-Term Access to Water 40

CHAPTER 6 *The Second Essential: Shelter*..**43**

    Where to Build Your Shelter...44

    Short Term Shelter Solutions 47

    Long-Term Shelter Solutions..48

CHAPTER 7 *The Third Essential: Fire* **53**

    Where to Build Your Fire..54

    Building a Birds Nest..55

    Fire for Heat...57

        Teepee Fire Lay 58

        Lean-to Fire Lay...59

        Log Cabin Fire Lay 60

        Long Burning Fire Lay 61

        Dakota Fire Pit 62

    Fire for Cooking...63

        Pyramid Fire Lay 63

        Star Fire With a Cooking Arm 64

CHAPTER 8 *The Fourth Essential: Food* **66**

    Types of Food to Eat in the Wilderness..67

    Foraging for Vegetation 68

    Hunting, Trapping, and Fishing 70

Butchering Small to Medium Game..72

Butchering Birds 74

Butchering Fish and Reptiles 76

Cleaning and Cooking Wild-Caught Meat 77

Properly Storing Food 78

Long-Term Gardening Solutions 80

CHAPTER 9 *The Fifth Essential: Safety* **82**

Protecting Yourself From Predators 84

Keeping Yourself and Your Camp Hygienic 86

First Aid Skills You Need to Know 90

  Treating Burns *90*

  Dressing Wounds *91*

  Setting Broken Bones *92*

  Dealing With Illness *94*

Foraging for Medicinal Plants *95*

CHAPTER 10 *The Great Escape* **96**

Escaping Minor Emergencies 97

Escaping Major Emergencies 98

CHAPTER 11 *The Unspoken Essential Of Survival* **101**

The Biggest Danger Lurking At Two AM 102

Keeping Yourself on Track for Survival 104

CHAPTER 12 *Getting Help When Needed* **106**

When Is the Right Time to Call? 107

Who Is the Right Person to Call? 109

How Can You Prepare to Be Rescued? 111

Is There Ever a Time When You Should Not Call? 112

CONCLUSION **114**

The Beginner's Vegetable Garden 2020

The Complete Beginner's Guide to Gardening and Survival in 2020

INTRODUCTION **118**

CHAPTER 1 *Raised Bed Gardening* **120**

- BASICS 122
  - *Sun* 123
  - *Drainage* 123
  - *Water* 124
  - *Logistics* 126
  - *Size* 127
- BUILDING STRUCTURES 129
  - *Materials Needed* 130
  - *Optional* 130
  - *Process* 130
  - *Various Structures* 131
  - *Garden Covers* 132
- PLANTS 133
  - *Plant Journal* 133
  - *Understanding the Plant Needs* 134
  - *Spacing* 134
  - *Companion Planting* 135
  - *Plants for Repelling Diseases and Pests* 135
  - *Combination for Improving Flavor* 137
  - *Best Combination for Raised Bed Garden* 137

- CROP ROTATION 138
  - *Reason for Crop Rotation* 138
  - *Crop Rotation Principles* 139
  - *Challenges for Raised Bed Crop Rotation* 139
  - *Sample Plan for Planting* 140
  - *Supplementing Garden Beds* 140
  - *Tips For Effective Crop Rotation* 140
- SOIL 141
  - *How Much Soil Is Required?* 142
  - *Best Soil for Raised Bed* 142
  - *Amending Soil Mixture* 143
  - *Maintenance* 144
- PLANTING 144
  - *Seeds* 145
  - *Where to Sow Seeds?* 145
- PROCESS OF SOWING SEEDS 146
  - *Planting Seedlings* 147
  - *Planting Seeds in Block* 147
- GROWING AND HARVESTING 148
  - *Watering* 148
  - *Paying Attention to Weather* 148
  - *Being Aware of the Watering Needs* 148
  - *Water During Morning* 149
  - *Thinning and Feeding Seedlings* 149
  - *Mulching* 149
  - *Fertilizing* 150
  - *Harvesting* 150
  - *Weeding* 150
- PEST CONTROL 151

CHAPTER 2 *Container Gardening* **153**

BASICS 155
Sun 156
Drainage 157
Water 159
Logistics 161
Size 161
Types of Containers 162

BUILDING STRUCTURES AND DESIGNS 163
Proportion 164
Focal Point 164
Designing With the Help of Edible Plants 165

PLANTS 165
Plant Journal 166
Spacing 166

PLANTS SUITABLE FOR CONTAINER GARDENING 166
Beans 167
Beets 167
Chard 167
Peppers 168
Companion Planting 168
Salad Mix 168
Root Vegetables 168
Tomatoes 169
Squash and Beans 169

CROP ROTATION 169
Simple Rotation of Crops 170
Rotating Crops According to Harvest Groups 170

 Crop Rotation With Plant Family *171*

Soil 172

 Choosing Soil for Potting *172*

 Best Soil for Gardening in Containers *173*

 Soil for Large Containers *174*

 Soil for Hanging Baskets *174*

 Reusing Container Soil *174*

Planting 175

 Sowing Seeds *175*

Process of Sowing Seeds 176

Growing and Harvesting 178

 Watering *178*

 Thinning *180*

 Mulching *181*

 Fertilizing *182*

 Harvesting *183*

 Weeding *183*

Pest Control 183

Pros & Cons 185

 Pros *185*

 Cons *186*

CHAPTER 3 *In-Ground Gardening* **187**

Basics 189

 Sun *189*

 Drainage *190*

 Water *191*

 Logistics *192*

 Size *192*

BUILDING STRUCTURES 194
    Materials Needed for Window Frame Trellis 194

PLANTS 195
    Plant Journal 196
    Spacing 196

COMPANION PLANTING 196
    Roses and Garlic 197
    Cabbage and Tomato 197
    Dill and Cabbage 197
    Beans and Corns 197
    Spinach and Radish 198

CROP ROTATION 198
    Plant Groups for Crop Rotation 199
    Crop Rotation and Its Benefits for In-Ground Gardening 200
    Planning Crop Rotation 200

SOIL 202
    Soil pH 202
    Soil Density 203
    Mix 203
    Maintenance 204

PLANTING 204
    Hill Method 205
    Trough Method 205

GROWING AND HARVESTING 206
    Watering 206
    Watering Less and Thoroughly 206
    Keep the Leaves Dry 207
    Avoid Waterlogging 207
    Thinning 207

- *Mulching* *208*
- *Fertilizing* *208*
- *Harvesting* *208*
- *Weeding* *209*

PEST CONTROL 210

PROS & CONS 211
- *Pros* *211*
- *Cons* *212*

CHAPTER 4 *Plant Profiles* 214

BASIL 214
- *Growing* *216*

BELL PEPPER 216
- *Starting* *217*
- *Growing* *217*

CABBAGE 218
- *Starting* *219*
- *Growing* *219*

BROCCOLI 220
- *Starting* *221*
- *Growing* *221*

BEET 222
- *Starting* *223*
- *Growing* *223*

CARROT 225
- *Starting* *226*
- *Growing* *226*

CILANTRO 227
- *Starting* *228*

  Growing *228*

 Chives 228

  Starting *229*

  Growing *230*

 Corn 230

  Starting *231*

  Growing *231*

 Onion 232

  Starting *233*

  Growing *233*

 Gardening Resources 234

CHAPTER 5 *List Of Common Gardening Terms* **235**

CHAPTER 6 *Companion Planting Guide* **240**

 Three Sisters 242

 Companion Planting Chart 244

CONCLUSION **250**

INTRODUCTION

Whether we like it or not, the affluent societies we have built for ourselves are not always as reliable as we need them to be. Our communities are made to be efficient. They were designed for everyday life in a modern world, so long as everyday life does not include any form of disaster that disrupts the system. The minute one small disaster strikes, though, the entire system can be thrown off course, and anywhere from hundreds to billions of people can be affected by the derailing of the system. This means that, despite how well it works on a good day, the system is unreliable, and you should *always* have a backup plan for when the system fails.

Backup plans can range from simple adjustments you can make to your everyday life to get through disruptions to your usual system and elaborate ideas for how you will escape and survive without any access to the modern system. And before you think, "I don't need something that elaborate!" I encourage you to think again. Natural disasters are increasingly common, with devastating fires, hurricanes, tornadoes, earthquakes, and even pandemics coming through and causing destruction for the populations they impact. In some cases, that destruction can be devastating and can lead to secondary injury, illness, or even death as people find themselves unable to access necessary resources like food, water, or shelter, or they become injured or killed by a damaged environment.

Knowing how to escape a dangerous situation and survive, no matter what the circumstances, is an important part of staying alive. As efficient as our system may be, if it fails, you must know how to survive on your own. With so many disasters that strike our society every year, you never know when one might strike you.

Learning how to survive is not nearly as challenging as you might think, though it does require some basic understanding of what you need to survive, and how you can safely acquire these resources. Clear guidance, combined with common sense and your built-in instincts will help you survive anything that might come your way.

If you are ready to discover how you can survive anything, let's begin.

CHAPTER 1

Essential Task List Of Survival

Surviving any situation requires you to know the five requirements of survival, and how you can safely secure those resources. Those who have never survived on their own must understand the importance of safely acquiring necessary resources without expending too much energy. In any survival situation, even minor ones, preserving energy and doing things in a logical manner is the best practice for securing your survival.

The essential task list of survival looks different depending on whether you are in a minor survival situation or a major disaster. In a small survival situation, you do not evacuate the premises so that you will be securing your survival from the comfort of your own home. In an extreme survival situation, you are required to evacuate the premises, so you will need to secure all of these things away from home, possibly in an off-grid situation. At home, emergencies can be classified as minor survivalist emergencies, whereas off-grid survival situations are major emergencies. If you find yourself away from home, but not in need of off-grid survival, you will want to select the survival practices that best fit your individual situation so you can survive in those unique circumstances.

No matter what your circumstances are, to secure your survival, you will require water, shelter, fire, food, and safety. The order in which you acquire these will depend on what stage you are in the unfolding emergency.

Minor Emergency Survival Task List

A minor emergency could be anything from an injury sustained at home, to a house fire, or other similar emergencies. Power outages, storms that make travel dangerous (but that do not affect your ability to stay home,) and other similar events are also minor emergencies. As the crisis is unfolding, you are in an active state of emergency. All minor emergencies, however, are usually isolated quickly, and you can move into a state of recovery rapidly. The exception may be in the instance of storms, such as winter storms, where you are unable to leave your home, so you must stay there. In these scenarios, you cannot guarantee when they will end, though the recovery from these storms is usually relatively quick and does not require evacuation.

If you find yourself in one of these situations, your task list for survival includes: secure safety, water, food, fire, and shelter, and get help.

Task #1: Secure Safety

Securing your safety is paramount in a situation where a minor emergency is unfolding. These emergencies can pose threats to your immediate safety, and if they are not mitigated, you could find the crisis growing more significant and more devastating by the minute. For example, if your house is on fire and you do not seek safety first, you run the risk of being burnt to death.

To effectively secure your safety, you need to ensure that you are aware of what the dangers are and who is around you so you can aid them in achieving their safety, too. However, you must never make the mistake of ensuring their safety *first*. If you are not safe, you will not be able to guarantee the safety of someone else. Often, in a state of panic, individuals will risk their safety to save someone else, only to put themselves in a dangerous situation where they are now both in need of being rescued by someone else. Sadly, this leads to many deaths. For example, if your friend were drowning in fast-moving water, it would not be safe for you to jump in to save them because rather than being able to save them, you, too, would begin drowning in fast moving water. It is extremely challenging to put your own safety above others' at times, but if you do not, you may find yourself also becoming extremely injured or even killed in a failed rescue mission.

To secure your safety, you must look at your surroundings, make a quick assessment of how safe you are in them, and then move to safer surroundings. For example, if you are in a burning house, it is evident that you are not safe, so you must immediately remove yourself from your surroundings. If you can bring your loved ones with you as you get out, do it. Once you are outside, you have reached safety and completed task number one.

Many minor emergencies require escaping a dangerous situation or calling for help to escape a hazardous situation. Some, however, may require you to stay in to avoid a dangerous situation. For example, in extreme winter storms, you may need to shut yourself in your house to protect yourself. In this case, your means of securing safety would be to ensure that all windows and doors are closed and that you have a generator to help you power your house through a possible power outage.

Task #2: Secure Water

Humans cannot survive longer than three to four days without water. When you are panicked, it may be the last thing you are thinking about, but you must stay hydrated if you want to remain healthy and alive. Getting access to clean, safe drinking water as soon as possible is an essential task. Being able to sip on water as you navigate a crisis, or the aftermath of one ensures you do not begin to suffer dehydration, and the many side effects dehydration brings with it. Realize that while you can survive three to four days without water, you will begin to deal with the symptoms of dehydration much sooner. This includes weakness, fatigue, dizziness, headaches, and other symptoms that can make survival much more challenging.

In minor emergencies, the best way to secure water is to already have water on hand. In your house, you likely already have access to tap water, and you may also have drinking water in your fridge. In case these resources run out or are not safe to consume in an emergency, it is also helpful to have bottled water or five-gallon jugs of water with a water dispenser. You will need three to four days' worth of water for every person in your house, including pets, in case of an emergency. You will need at least 3 liters of drinking water per person and animal in your family. You should also have water available for other purposes, such as cleaning, sterilizing your environment, or bathing. This means if you have a family of four plus one dog and one cat, you will need 18 liters of drinking water, plus about 40 to 60 liters of water for other uses such as cleaning. It may sound like a lot, but the average human uses about 80 to 100 gallons of water per day, between bathing, flushing the toilet, washing their hands and brushing their teeth, doing the dishes, and engaging in other water-related activities. Reduce your consumption by using fewer flushes, sharing bathwater, and using wash basins rather than running water, as these will all conserve water.

Task #3: Secure Food

The third task you must secure is food. Humans can survive up to three weeks without food, but the longer you go, the more symptoms you will endure, which will make securing and consuming food far more challenging. In a minor emergency, having access to smaller food items is a great way to ensure you provide yourself with everything you need to stay well-nourished. Having a well-stocked pantry, fridge, and freezer helps, too.

It is advised that you keep two to four weeks' worth of food in your home. You can also keep snack bars, trail mix, beef jerky, and other small, non-perishable, nutrient-dense snacks in emergency locations, such as in your car, to ensure proper nutrition during dangerous situations. You would be surprised how hungry you get within minutes or hours of moving out of an active state of emergency and into the recovery phase. Getting nutrients into your body helps you recover from the intense energy demands that the emergency itself placed on your body.

Task #4: Secure Fire

Securing fire may or may not be necessary in minor emergencies. In something isolated, like an injury, fire is likely completely unnecessary. In something such as a power outage, though, securing fire is important. Fire is used for heat to keep your core temperature stable, as well as for cooking. In minor emergencies, replace open fires with electricity, gas ovens, or propane-fueled barbecues for cooking. Insulated clothes and blankets can be used to maintain a proper body temperature. If you are out of electricity and do not have access to a safe fuel source, you can also start a small fire in a homemade pit in your backyard to help you stay warm and cook food with.

Inside of your home, the best way to keep yourself warm is to light candles, pile as many blankets together as you can, and wear warm woolen clothes that are designed to keep you warm. If you are in an extreme situation and cannot get warm, wear a thin layer of clothes, or no clothes, under a blanket with other people so your body temperature can work together to help heat each other up.

Task #5: Secure Shelter

In most minor emergencies, you can stay in your home or somewhere close to home. For example, in the event of a flood or fire, you may have to leave your home, but your town would be perfectly safe for you to stay in. The emergency you are in will decide what needs to be done to protect your shelter in that emergency.

If you are able to stay inside of your house, securing shelter means ensuring that your shelter is safe for you to stay in. This could mean locking doors, or closing and locking windows. You might also need to secure outdoor furniture, so it doesn't blow around and cause harm. If you are in the middle of a winter storm, you may need to close off the doors to the main room in your home, cover the bottom of those doors with towels to prevent heat from escaping, and focus on heating that primary area of your house. The entire key is to ensure that the space you are surviving in is capable of keeping you protected from the elements while giving you adequate space to fulfill your other four basic needs.

Task #6: Get Help

Finally, if you are in an emergency, the minute everything is stabilized, you may need to call for help. Unless it is a minor injury or something else that is relatively small and can be secured at home, without additional help, you will need to be prepared to call for assistance with getting your situation remedied.

A vital step to take *before* you ever reach the point where you need to get help is to have the contact information for anyone who may assist you through any emergency present and easy-to-access at all times. A list on the fridge, for example, is a great way to have these numbers available. Include the local emergency number, authorities, doctors and dentist numbers, poison control, and other essential emergency numbers on your list. You should also include numbers for your personal identification and your health insurance policy, dates of birth, in case any of this is required in an emergency phone call.

Major Emergency Survival Task List

If you are in a major emergency survival situation, the approach is going to be much different. In major emergencies, you can be driven out of your home with very little time to prepare, and you may need to survive in the wilderness for an extended period of time. Knowing how to protect yourself and your family in these types of emergencies is important. It is also where many people are largely unprepared and find themselves making serious mistakes that can lead to injury, illness, or even death. We will cover all of these tasks in far greater detail later in this book, but for now, you need to know what these tasks are and what order they fall in.

Task #1: Secure Water

The first task you must fulfill immediately upon escaping a dangerous situation is securing water. You can only survive three to four days without water, but after one day, you can start experiencing serious side effects from not being hydrated enough. Since it can take some time to access and purify water for drinking in the wilderness, you need to make it your number one priority to find some. This way, if it takes you a day or more to find any water sources, you have enough time actually to find them before dehydration ultimately proves fatal.

Another benefit of securing water first, aside from it saving your life, is that you know where the water is and can build your camp near the water source so that it is easy for you to access that water source continually.

Task #2: Secure Shelter

Securing shelter should always be your second move after obtaining water. Your shelter should be close enough to water so that it is easy to access, but not so close that the water poses a threat itself. Your goal with shelter in off-grid survivalist situations is to create a shelter that maintains your core temperature, keeps you comfortable, and provides you with safety from the elements. This means you will need to build it away from widowmakers, or environmental dangers that can instantly kill you if they are triggered, and in such a way that fulfills your needs for shelter.

If you were able to bring supplies with you, a shelter can easily be built out of tarps and rope. If you were not, you will have to use elements of the environment to build your shelter. The environment features many resources you can use to create high-quality, lasting shelter in any situation. For example, trees, branches, mud, leaves, stones, and even snow can be used to create a shelter for yourself, depending on what situation you are in. As long as it can protect you from the elements and provide a safe space for you to stay warm in, it is plenty for your shelter.

Task #3: Secure Fire

After you have secured your shelter, you need to secure fire. Fire is used in an abundance of ways in off-grid survival situations. Fire provides warmth, a means for cooking, and a way to sterilize your tools and yourself. There are many reasons you will use fire in a survival situation, so be prepared to know how to create adequate fire lays for any circumstance. In the wilderness, there are many options for the types of fires you can build. You will need to know how to build a variety of fires, as they will all support you with keeping yourself safe. Specific fire lays can be used to keep you warm overnight, heat your camp for a few hours, cook, or alert others to your whereabouts through smoke signals. Each fire lay is also designed to prevent your fire from growing out of control to ensure you do not accidentally start a forest fire.

Task #4: Secure Food

If you have time on the day of your arrival in your survivalist location, you will want to secure food. If it is later in the day or into the evening, though, you will want to wait as food can take a while to secure. Starting on day two, focus all your efforts on securing food as you will need as many calories as possible to sustain yourself in the wilderness. You will need a variety of foraged vegetation and meat to keep yourself going, especially in the wilderness, as the protein will be important for keeping your energy up and allowing you to survive the pressure being placed on your body.

With securing food, you will also need to secure a means for cooking and preserving that food. In the wilderness, this requires additional measures you must take to prevent predators from hunting you based on the scents you are creating through the foods you are cooking. Especially as you kill, cook, and store meat, you will be at risk of attracting predators who may try to steal your meat from you. Proper safety measures will ensure you can accomplish all of this without harming yourself or losing your bounty to another predator.

Task #5: Secure Safety

Safety is paramount in survivalist situations, especially when you are off-grid. Off-grid, you do not have access to things like doctors, emergency responders, police, firefighters, or anyone else who can help you out of a dangerous situation. You must place safety first so you can prevent hazardous situations from arising, hopefully meaning you never actually need emergency support in your survivalist situation. If you do, keep safety kits available to help you deal with any emergencies you may face. These emergency kits ensure you can navigate any situation safely and successfully.

Task #6: Get Help

After you have secured your survival, you need to get help. This might include traveling into cell service, finding your way back to a major civilization where someone can help you, or even using flares or smoke signals to indicate where you are if a search and rescue team is searching for you. Getting help is important, as help is how you will be able to ultimately get yourself out of this situation and back into a safe civilized location.

There are, however, times where you may not be able to call for help. For example, if you are escaping a police state or a major emergency like a pandemic, it may not be feasible for you to call for help. Unfortunately, people often find themselves in situations where they cannot or should not rely on the help that would otherwise be available to them. In these scenarios, those who may claim to help you might actually cause more harm than they would solve. In this case, you would omit calling for help and instead begin focusing on tasks that will set you up for long-term survival.

CHAPTER 2

On-Grid Survival Guide

The on-grid survival guide is undoubtedly the more comfortable survival guide to follow. On-grid, many tools exist to help you meet your survival needs. You should leverage them in every way possible, as they will minimize the amount of energy you have to exert while also keeping your habits as close to normal as possible. If you can, lean on corporate resources to stock yourself up with everything you need to survive. All you need to do, then, is know how to do this efficiently and effectively to secure your survival.

One thing I cannot stress enough is the importance of knowing that you are responsible for your own survival. In an emergency, you may find yourself wanting to wait for the government or public health officials to direct you on what to do and where to go. The problem with this is that it could take hours, days, or even weeks for them to organize everything and get enough resources to sustain everyone effectively. In the meantime, you could be floundering as you have not been able to access the resources you need. While relying on this system to get more resources is helpful, it is important that you have your own plan in place so that you are not waiting for someone else to promise you your safety. Instead, you can take it into your own hands and secure your safety and the safety of your family, which will result in your successful survival.

Short-Term VS. Long-Term On-Grid Survival

Short-term on-grid survival and long-term on-grid survival both look the same; however, you will need more supplies for long-term survival than you will for short-term survival. Most on-grid survival situations will be short-term. Some, however, may be long-term. For example, amid the pandemic of 2020, many were forced to self-isolate or stay home for extended periods without direct and consistent access to necessary resources, such as grocery stores or their general health practitioners. Another example of long-term on-grid survival would be if you lived in a place where winters were severe, and power could be out for days or even weeks on end, or if the harsh weather eliminated your ability to access resources such as the grocery store.

For long-term survival situations, you need to have an abundance of water, food, and heat sources available at a moment's notice, or the ability to quickly access it if you do not have any readily available. You also need to have the ability to defend yourself, administer basic health-care needs if necessary, and secure your shelter. Ideally, you should have enough to protect yourself for up to one month. However, you may prefer to have more if you will be in a situation where you know accessing resources will be nearly impossible for extended periods.

Securing Safety

Securing your safety on-grid starts with assessing your environment, identifying possible hazards, and protecting yourself from any impending dangers. In obvious cases, such as during a fire or flood, this means escaping the affected building and getting yourself into a safe space. In less obvious situations, though, this requires more extensive care and attention.

In any environment, there can be a wide number of dangers threatening yourself or your family. Complete an assessment of your environment by quickly studying everything for obvious risks, then scanning from the ground up since most hazards are at ground-level. In your home, this could include stoves, electric outlets, fallen furniture, or other common household hazards. Outside, this might include power lines, traffic, fallen trees, weather, or other landscape or natural hazards. Always be aware of what the likely dangers are in your area, as this allows you to scan in an educated manner and avoid accidental illness, injury, or death.

Be highly aware of anything that could be classified as a widowmaker. Widowmakers are not always apparent at first, but they do have the power to instantly injure or kill a person who came into contact with them. For example, a fallen powerline, broken gas lines, or exposure to chemicals are incredibly unsafe. If you suspect there may be something dangerous in your environment, rectify it, or remove yourself from the situation immediately. Hazards can rapidly turn into actual emergencies without any warning. It is better to remove yourself and your family from the area than to hope it will not become a hazard and find out later that you were wrong. When in doubt, never take a risk that comes with a possible consequence that you would not want to face.

As soon as you have assessed your situation, you need to either remove safety hazards or take necessary measures to remove yourself from the vicinity of those dangers if they are not able to be fixed safely. Safely is the keyword here, as you should never attempt to resolve a hazard by yourself if you are not confident that you can do it by yourself, and sure that you have the necessary tools to do it yourself. If you lack the necessary tools or the know-how, you need to wait for someone more experienced to resolve the safety hazard and instead focus on keeping yourself away from it so it cannot pose a threat to your safety or livelihood. This may mean leaving a certain area, leaving a building altogether, or otherwise moving somewhere safer so that you are no longer at risk of being injured or killed by that hazard.

Securing Water

The easiest way to secure water in an on-grid survival situation is to turn on your tap. In most minor emergencies, accessing water from your taps is still possible. You could then drink it, or run it through a purifying system you already have on hand if you live in a location where water purifiers are needed. If accessing tap water was not possible, though, such as if your water was turned off, a line busted, and you could not receive water through the lines, or your water was contaminated, the next best thing is to buy water.

Water bottles and five-gallon jugs of water are the best way to go, as they ensure you have enough water to get through an emergency. If you are unable to source any, you can also collect rainwater, water from a natural body of water, or uncontaminated snow, and purify it. It is vital that you purify this water properly, however, as they are all likely to have contaminants in them, especially if you are in an urban environment with a high-density population. These areas are known for being highly polluted, which makes them a threat to your health.

Securing Food

Like with securing water, securing food in an on-grid survival setting should be as easy as going to the grocery store and getting some, ideally, you should have at least two weeks to one month's worth of food in your pantry at any given time so that you have plenty to get you through in case accessing the grocery store becomes challenging. If you run out of food at home, you may be able to rely on a local charitable organization to provide you with food until you can secure more. However, some emergencies may lead to you being unable to secure food from these sources.

If you cannot secure food from the grocery store or a local organization, the best thing you can do is turn to fishing or trapping. Fishing is generally legal in most places, while trapping may or may not be legal, depending on where you are. You may need permits to do either activity, though. Avoid hunting in cities or townships, as it would be easy for you to accidentally hurt another person, rather than the animal you were targeting, and that would be devastating. Further, it could bring with it major charges and prison time, which would make an emergency even more devastating for everyone involved.

Securing Fire

Securing fire benefits three primary things associated with your survival. Fire maintains your core temperature, helps you cook, and allows you to adequately sterilize things in your environment through either smoke or boiling water. In an urban environment, actual fire may not be necessary as you may be able to secure these three things in different ways. For example, if you have access to electricity, a stove or barbecue, and washing agents, you should not need to have a fire to secure these elements. If, however, you cannot access electricity, a stove, or a barbecue, you may need to improvise.

The order of improvising should be as follows: if you cannot rely on electricity from your main power source, turn on a generator. If you cannot rely on a generator, turn to a fuel source like propane barbecues or coal-based barbecues. If you cannot rely on a barbecue, turn to candles and fire pits or fireplaces. You can also use warm clothes and blankets to keep your space warm. For cooking, you may be able to eat food items that you can get from the grocery store that does not require cooking, such as cereal, granola bars, beef jerky, fruits and vegetables, bread, and other items that do not need to be cooked. For sterilizing, you can always use cleaning agents such as soap or cleaning products to keep your environment sterile and healthy.

Securing Shelter

Securing shelter should be the easiest thing to do in a minor emergency where you are able to remain on-grid. In most emergencies, even long-term emergencies, you should be able to stay safe inside your home. Ideally, your home should have everything a shelter needs for you to remain safe and secure throughout the emergency. If your home is not an option, you can always stay with a family member or a friend. If that is not an option, you can look into emergency shelters and housing facilities put on by your city, as these locations can often provide you a place to stay until you are able to return to your own home.

CHAPTER 3

Off-Grid Survival Guide

Off-grid survival is far more challenging, requires more energy and effort on your behalf, and takes preparation and know-how. If you have never had to survive off-grid, you likely cannot imagine the amount of work and energy it requires for you to be able to preserve your life in an off-grid environment. Despite how much work it takes, you will be pleased to know that in survival situations, your body is designed with all of the chemicals and hormones you require to stay alert, navigate dangers, and keep yourself going through any problems you face. Still, you need to know what to do and how to do it so that all of your energy and enthusiasm can be applied toward something that will actually turn results.

Surviving off-grid requires far more than I can put in one chapter, so we are first going to discuss what needs to be done for you to survive off-grid. Then, we will discuss all of these measures in far greater detail, complete with tutorials and step-by-step instructions, in later chapters. This way, your mind is organized and ready to receive this knowledge, and you receive the step-by-step guidance you need to put it to work.

The Preparation Before the Emergency

Preparing for an emergency before one actually strikes is the most valuable thing you can do for yourself. Do not fail to prepare because you believe you would never face an emergency, because then when you do, you will not be prepared. Have everything ready so that if something does go wrong, you are prepared for that situation. Many people mistakenly believe that it cannot happen to them, but the reality is that minor and major emergencies alike can strike anyone at any time. None of us are exempt from the dangers lurking in everyday life. Preparation ensures that you have everything you need to survive any one of those dangers, should they strike.

To prepare for your emergency, you need to have the necessary tools and resources readily available, as well as knowledge on how to use those tools and support if need be. This includes having adequate supplies for water, shelter, fire, food, and safety on hand at all times, and knowing exactly how to use all of those tools to get the most out of them. The better you are at preparing, the more ready you will be in the event of an emergency.

Your preparation will come in two parts. The first will include preparing your tools. Your tools will all be bought, gathered, and stored in grab N go bags or G'nG bags, which are designed to make it easy for you to quickly grab all of the necessary tools and evacuate if need be. These should be ready even for minor emergencies that occur at your home, as they will be full of every tool you need to navigate those emergencies. You will also want to have money set aside. If you do find that you need money to navigate a more significant crisis. This way, if you are unable to work for an extended period of time, you do not go bankrupt trying to afford life in the meantime.

Aside from preparing your tools, educate yourself on how they work and when to use them. You should also be trained on how to observe wear and tear, damage, or expiration signs on the tools so that you can replace them. You will want to replace tools as needed in your emergency kit, even if they are going unused, to ensure you have new, useable tools in the event of an emergency.

Securing Your Five Needs for Survival

Preparation is all you will need unless an emergency arises. In the event that an emergency arises, you need to escape your environment and secure your five needs for survival, or your water, shelter, fire, food, and safety. Escaping should be seen as an essential safety measure in your first five, as remaining in an area that has an active emergency is highly dangerous and can lead to injury, illness, or death. We will go into far greater detail on your five needs for survival and how to practically secure each one, as well as how to escape to a safer environment, later.

Setting Your Short-Term Survival Expectations

Your short-term expectations in the wilderness should include having everything you need to get through a few days until help can get to you and bring you to safety, or until it is safe for you to return home. You will likely live in a shelter made of tarps and ground cloths, eat whatever food you were able to deliver with you, and possibly fish or forage for some additional food and drink through whatever water you were able to bring. Depending on your circumstance, you may need to locate and purify water, too. Building fire should also be comfortable enough with whatever fuel sources you brought with you.

Aside from the emergency aspect and the stress and trauma, it can bring with it, surviving in the wilderness for a few days is not unlike taking a camping trip. Although it was not a planned camping trip, and it certainly will not feel relaxing based on the circumstances, the same skills are required, and the same expectations around what it takes to survive will fit this situation, too.

Setting Your Long-Term Survival Expectations

Long-term survival expectations are far more challenging to set, though they are essential as knowing what to expect helps you prepare and endure that situation if you find yourself in it. In a long-term situation, you need to be ready to create more elaborate accommodations to support your survival. Tarp tents and fishing and foraging are unlikely to be enough in this situation. As well, you will likely not want to have to go fill and purify your canteen of water several times a day, every single day. You need to be ready to set yourself up with an elaborate living condition that can sustain you for as long as you need.

Your shelter in long-term survival situations will likely be made of wood, branches, brush, leaves, clay, dirt, and other findings that you can use from the environment to create a warm and comfortable dwelling that keeps you safe from the elements. You will also likely set up a more efficient cooking camp, proper storage measures for your food, and a place where you can gather and store water so that you do not have to fetch it so often. Long-term storage of wood for your fire, as well as tools for preserving your safety, are important. Eventually, predators will come to know where you are and may become more curious about you and what is going on, and you will need to protect yourself from those predators. As far as food goes, hunting and trapping will be useful in long-term survival situations, as well as gardening.

CHAPTER 4

Necessary Survival Materials

Since preparation is key to success in surviving any situation, you need to ensure that you are prepared at all times. Preparing for survival means having the right materials on hand so that you can navigate any situation with adequate tools. While many tools can be made in the bush, it is often easier to have your own that were made to fulfill specific needs, as they will be more effective and will result in better outcomes. The tools you need will cover everything that has to be done in the wilderness, ranging from traveling to get there or traveling through the wilderness, to securing water, shelter, fire, food, and safety.

In addition to gathering the necessary tools, you need to keep them neatly organized in G'n'G bags so they can quickly be grabbed during an emergency evacuation. This way, you are not scrambling to find all of your tools and put them together in the event that something goes wrong. You also need to review your materials on a regular basis to ensure that they are working, that they still meet current safety standards, and that they have not expired or otherwise sustained damage that makes them unusable.

Tools for Water

For water, you need tools that will allow you to carry and store it, as well as tools that will allow you to purify it.

- Water bottles and storage containers
- Cups
- Water purifying containers
- Water purifying drops

Tools for Shelter

For shelter, you need tools that will enable you to build a well-designed camp. Your shelter will need to be able to protect you from all of the elements, while also offering comfort. You want a shelter that will be easy to design, too, so you are not wasting any energy or frustration over building a shelter for yourself and anyone who is staying at the camp with you.

- Rope and cordage

- Tarps and tarp tents
- Polypropylene
- Silnylon
- Canvas
- Oilcloth
- Ground pads
- Browse bags
- Emergency thermal blankets
- Hammock
- Sleeping bags
- Military modular sleeping system
- Wool blankets
- Saw

Tools for Fire

For fire, you will need devices that will allow you to start a fire, as well as fuel for those devices. You may also need fuel for the fire itself if you are having a hard time getting your fire going.

- Lighters
- Ferrocerium rods
- Magnifying glass
- Ax

- Charring tins
- Fire starters (cotton, cardboard, lint from the dryer, etc.)

Tools for Food

Tools for food will include tools for hunting, cleaning, cooking, eating, and storing your food. The best tools are ones that allow you to accomplish many different tasks with that single tool, as this ensures you are not having to pack so many different things with you into the bush or around on hunting, trapping, or fishing trips.

- Knives
- Swiss Army Knife
- Whetstone
- Grinds
- Pots
- Skillet
- Meat rotisserie
- Planks
- Cast iron
- Cooking irons
- Stoves and burners
- Fishing wire
- Fish hooks
- Fishing rod (optional, a stick can be used if needed)

- Snare lines
- Bait
- Plates, bowls, and eating utensils
- Cooking utensils
- Stainless steel food storage containers
- Salt

Tools for Safety

Tools for safety include tools that will allow you to protect yourself in your camp, as well as tools that can be used in first aid situations. A well-stocked first-aid kit is important and should be in your G'n'G bag at all times.

- Bar soap
- Toothpaste
- Towels
- Bear spray
- Bear bangers
- First aid kit
    - 25 adhesive bandages in assorted sizes
    - 2 absorbent compress dressings (5 x 9 inches)
    - 2 triangular bandages
    - 1 adhesive cloth tape (10 yards x 1 inch)
    - 5 antiseptic wipes in individual packages

- 5 antibiotic ointment packets
- 2 packets of aspirin
- 2 hydrocortisone ointment packets
- 1 breathing barrier with a one-way valve
- 1 emergency blanket
- 1 instant cold compress
- 2 pairs of disposable gloves
- 1 3-inch gauze roll bandage
- 1 roller bandage, 4 inches wide
- 5 3 x 3-inch sterile gauze pads
- Oral thermometer (non-mercury and non-glass)
- Tweezers
- Emergency first aid guide
- Emergency radio

Tools for Travel

Tools for travel include all devices that will allow you to easily pack your materials into the bush. They also include all tools that will allow you to pack your materials through the forest, such as if you need to bring some things with you to forage, hunt, or fish for food.

- Bushcrafting backpack
- Bushcrafting vest (one for each person, properly sized)
- Canvas bags

- Smaller bags for organizing different things with (reusable shopping bags, small canvas bags, drawstring bags, etc.)

CHAPTER 5

The First Essential: Water

The very first thing you must have when escaping to the wilderness is to get there safely. We will discuss effective escaping methods in Chapter 10: The Great Escape. Once you have safely arrived at your survival location, you need to be able to access water. It is important that locating and accessing water is your first order of business, as this is going to enable you to find the perfect location to set your camp up in relation to the water. You always want to have your camp near water, even if you will only be there for a short period of time because it allows you to quickly and easily access the water itself. Water can be heavy, and hauling it back and forth from a water source to your camp can be exhausting and can expend energy that would be better used elsewhere.

Locating and Accessing Water

Hopefully, before you ever had to escape an urban situation, you had already surveyed a location for you to survive in, should the need arise. If not, however, it is relatively easy to source water in the bush. In the bush, you will be looking for a river, stream, or waterfall as these are all rapid-moving bodies of water that are likely to have fewer diseases and parasites in them. Lakes, ponds, marshes, and puddles should all be very last resorts, as they are likely full of disease and parasites since they cannot be filtered as easily as moving bodies of water can be. You can also catch rainwater in a container if you are in an area where rainfall is abundant. If you are in a dire situation, you can also look for an area that has fairly moist ground, and then you can try digging until you find water, however, there is no guarantee that this will work and it will expend a large amount of energy. As well, just because water is moving does not mean it is clean and safe for you to drink. You will need to purify your water with purifying drops, a purifying filter, or at the very least, by boiling it for 10 minutes before consuming it. Even moving water can be contaminated, and contamination can lead to illness or even death in unfortunate circumstances.

To source a moving body of water, take a look at the landscape around you. Particularly dry plants suggest that you are in an area where water is further away. If you can spot vegetation that is known for growing closer to water, such as mint, cattails, or ferns, you are likely close to a body of water. In this case, follow this patch of plants until you locate the water that they are growing around. Another great way to find water is to look for animal trails. Animals require water to survive. Well-worn paths in the forest indicate that you have located an "animal highway," or popular animal trail. Follow these trails to locate a water source. Look at the foliage to ensure that you are walking toward the water and not away from it.

If you do not rapidly come across a body of water, the next best thing to do is stop searching for water and start searching for altitude. Start walking up the highest piece of landscape you see, that you can reasonably walk up. Once you are well above the lower terrain, you will be able to look out across the land and get your bearings. You should be able to see water from this point, either through the body of water itself, or the clear distinction of well-hydrated vegetation. Again, it should be quite obvious as it will appear well-hydrated and deep green in color. Once you spot water, pinpoint landmarks, so you know exactly which direction to walk in order to get to the water. When you begin walking, ensure that you follow these milestones exactly, so you do not find yourself lost.

If you are still unable to source water, the next thing you must do is track animals. Be slow and steady, as animals will flee if they think they are being tracked, as they will believe you are hunting them. Taking your time and following the animals carefully will almost always lead you to a body of water, as animals will visit water several times per day to stay hydrated, since animals require hydration, too. While tracking animals, be very aware of your surroundings as remaining too focused on the animals you are tracking could leave you vulnerable to exposure, either with dangerous landscape features or with other animals who may be simultaneously tracking you.

Purifying and Storing Water

Properly purifying your water and storing it is essential. Failure to purify your water can lead to you consuming contaminated water and falling ill or being infected with parasites. Failing to store your water safely can lead to new contaminants being introduced to your water, which can also result in you falling ill. For short term survival situations, a large stainless steel water bottle or canteen is plenty for storing your water with. You should have one container per person, but containers can be shared if you were unable to bring more with you. You will simply need to refill the container more frequently to ensure everyone has access to adequate water.

Purifying your water can be done four different ways in the bush. Filtered bottles or purifying drops or tablets are the most common short term water purifying solutions in the bush, as they will instantly purify your water and protect you from contaminants. Both of these items can be purchased from a camping supply store or a military supply store, and they can be safely stored within your G'n'G gear for extended periods.

If you do not have access to purifying devices, there are two additional methods you can use for purifying your water in the bush. The preferred method is by fashioning a filter using materials from nature, while the latter is used in any purifying circumstance but can work on its own in a pinch. To create your own filter, take a cotton t-shirt and lay it over the top of a stainless steel pot. Then, you will take charcoal out of the bottom of your campfire and make a generous layer over the cotton shirt. If you can, have someone holding the shirt taut, so it covers the top of the pot, without falling in or having your filter tools fall off. Next, you will layer small gravel, dirt, and finally grass over the shirt. Then, you will pour water through this shirt, and it will land into the pot below. While you could technically drink this water now, it is possible that it is still contaminated, so it is best to boil the water afterward. Which, by the way, is the last option for purifying your water. Boiling your water on a heavy-rolling boil for at least 10 minutes ensures that it is safe enough for your consumption. Do not boil it for any less than that, and ensure that it remains on a full rolling boil so that you safely kill off any bacteria or parasites that may be contaminating your water. If you were unable to store your water in an airtight container, you will need to do this anytime you are about to drink it as new parasites or bacteria could be introduced to improperly stored water.

The proper storage solution for purified water is an airtight stainless steel bottle or canteen, as these will keep your water safe for drinking. You may need to purify water frequently if you only have small storage bottles, though you can always store larger amounts close to camp, so you do not have to haul water back so frequently. This way, while you still have to boil the water consistently, you are not wasting energy going back and forth to the water source several times per day or week.

Building Your Camp Near a Body of Water

Once you have located a water source, you need to decide where you will set up camp. It is important to concern yourself with this factor before doing much else, as this will help you decide where you will set up your fire and get yourself situated so that you can purify your water. Your camp should always be above the water line, and away from water runoffs enough that the ground will not be wet where you are camping. A wet ground can rapidly lead to illness, as it keeps you wet and damp for long periods of time, which is dangerous for your health. Your feet and face, especially, need to be kept dry. Excessive moisture around your face or feet can lead to infections. In the facial area, you run the risk of respiratory infection, whereas, around the feet, you run the risk of gangrene. Both can be fatal.

You also need to keep your camp away from the most common wildlife corridor. Bodies of water will always attract wildlife, and if you are not careful, you may place yourself on active trails, which can lead to you getting far too many wild visitors to your camp. While wildlife is unavoidable in the wilderness, you can situate yourself away from the main trails and corridors to ensure you are not directly in a busy place for wildlife to visit. You can tell if an area is busy for wildlife because you will notice a large amount of scat, fur, scratch marks, broken branches, and other signs that this is a place that is frequented by many critters.

If you build your camp uphill from a body of water, build your camp far enough back that if a landslide happened, you would not fall into the water or be crushed in the process. Soil erosion can lead to water banks being rather finicky, and if you are too close to a water bank, the weight of you walking along that space can result in the bank giving out and you falling in. This could lead to many dangers, ranging from hypothermia to drowning, or other water-related illnesses, injuries, or deaths.

Lastly, you need to consider how your water is going to be accessed and brought back to your camp. Based on where you have situated yourself, is it easy for you to take a large pot or basin down to the water source and bring it back to camp? You can guarantee this by looking for a trail that is easy to access and following that trail down to the water. Then, you need to consider how capable you will be of bringing the water back to camp, and how safe it will be for you to do so. Be careful about wildlife and soil erosion when collecting water, too, as something as simple as walking up an eroding bank or past unexpecting wildlife can lead to injuries or fatalities. If it is reasonable for you to access the water, the water does not pose a threat, and you have considered all other circumstances, you have found the perfect location for building your camp.

Securing Long-Term Access to Water

For long-term survival, you need to set up long-term access to water. This means you need to have a large, steady supply of water coming in that can be purified in large batches and stored safely so that it can be consumed. There are several ways that you can ensure safe access to drinking water, though many of these ways will require you to have proper storage containers for you to use in these situations. We will discuss options for if you have an abundance of tools or resources at your disposal, as well as options for if you don't so that you know how you can safely store water for long periods of time.

If you have an abundance of resources on hand, you can store water rather easily. Carrying larger containers of water from your water source back to camp, purifying them, and storing them in stainless steel, aluminum, high-density polyethylene (HDPE) containers, or uncracked glass containers enables you to store large amounts of water at once. This way, you can fetch, purify, and store water a few times a week rather than a few times a day, which saves plenty of time, energy, and resources.

If the area you are staying in experiences high amounts of rainfall, you can also collect rainwater for purifying. Rainwater tends to be cleaner than other water sources because it came straight from the sky and never had the chance to settle and become contaminated with things on the ground, or animals who may have interacted with it once it reached the ground. With that being said, you will need a rather large container to reasonably capture rainwater in, or at least several smaller containers that are capturing rainwater. You will also need to have access to a spot that is not covered by trees or brush so that the containers are directly exposed to the sky. If your water is falling through the trees first, it may become contaminated by bird feces, animals who are living in the trees, or other contaminants that could find their way into your water source. When it is not actively raining, you should cover your rain barrels to prevent contamination from vegetation, bugs, and animals.

If you do not have containers that you can store water in for extended periods of time, the next best thing you can do is set up a system for purifying your water each morning. Keep your homemade charcoal filter readily available next to a pot near your stove or the fire, as well as extra charcoal from the fire available for filtration. Then, each morning, your first order of business should be to collect water for the day. Go early enough that it is not too hot, but not so early that you encounter all of the wildlife accessing their first morning drink, which will likely happen around dawn and for an hour or two after. Once you have gathered your water, bring it back, filter it, and consume your water. Each evening, keep one or two containers filled with enough water for everyone and sterilize the other ones in boiling water. Rotate which ones are being sterilized in the evening to ensure they are both receiving adequate cleanings between usages.

It may take more work to access and store your water this way, but water is a non-negotiable when it comes to survival. Working into an efficient system ensures that you have access to all of the water you need, without having to expend any added energy getting it. This also ensures that you never miss a step and that you never go without.

In long-term survival situations, if you have purifying drops or tablets on hand, they should be preserved for dire circumstances, rather than used at camp. At camp, use a homemade charcoal filter and boiling method for purifying your water in large quantities. The filter or purifying drops and tablets can be preserved for days when you may need to venture away from camp, such as for fishing or hunting. This way, you do not have to transport an excess of fire starting materials and pots around with you to purify your water on the go.

CHAPTER 6

The Second Essential: Shelter

As soon as you have secured water, you need to secure a place to build your shelter, too. Your shelter, as you know, should be relatively close to a body of water, but not so close that it becomes hazardous. Aside from that, there are many other things to consider when it comes to building your shelter. Hardy individuals will advise that your shelter is merely a place to lay your head at night and that you should not think too much about it. I don't believe this is adequate advice, as it ignores the notion that our shelters are often our homes, and our homes provide a great sense of comfort and relief when they are built appropriately. In a normal, everyday situation, your home is where you live, and it provides you with a sense of comfort and security to live there, which is why you are able to unwind and tend to your mental and emotional needs. In the wilderness, your shelter will serve as your home for as long as you need it to, and you require it to offer the same mental and emotional solace. Being able to nurture your own mind and emotions in a survival situation is imperative, as it prevents you from running yourself into total burnout and then failing to have the energy required to get through the situation at hand.

Aside from the fact that your shelter should be properly built and designed in such a way that provides security, comfort, and relief, there are many other things that need to be factored into the building process. How much effort you put into it and what you do to build your shelter will depend on how long you will be surviving there for, and what materials you have available for you. If you were able to escape with a well-packed G'n'G bag, you should have plenty of tools you can rely on to help set up your camp. These tarps, ground covers, ropes and cordages, axes, and other materials will make building your shelter far easier. If you did not escape with your G'n'G bag, or if tools are missing out of it, you can make an adequate shelter out of everything in the bush, so there is no need to worry if you had to escape and were unable to bring your tools with you, or if you later realized your tools were inadequate or damaged.

Where to Build Your Shelter

The first thing you must be aware of when it comes to building your shelter is knowing where to build it. You already know how to situate your shelter near a body of water, but there are many other things to consider, too. The wilderness can pose many dangers that you need to consider if you are going to be able to safely survive for any period. Build shelter away from immediate dangers, as well as less-obvious dangers, to avoid harming anyone at your camp. Improperly located shelters can and do, lead to serious injuries and even fatalities. It may sound excessive if you have never been in the wilderness, but it is a reality, and unfortunately, it hurts and injures thousands every year. Anything from falling trees to wildlife and other dangers can present themselves and result in fatalities in the bush, which is directly contradictory to your desire to survive.

Finding the best place to set up your camp requires you to know about widowmakers or dangers that can instantly kill anyone in your camp, including yourself. In the bush, the most common widowmaker is a tree or tree branch that has begun falling down but has yet to fall all the way down. Dead trees also pose a danger, as they are weak and can easily be blown over or broken in various weather conditions, which can lead to them falling. If you were to build your shelter under or even near this tree or tree branch, it could fall at any time and instantly injure or kill anyone who was under it. It is imperative that you look around at the trees surrounding you when you are building your shelter, and when you are moving around the wilderness in general, so you can steer clear of potential hazards such as falling trees or tree branches. As well, never underestimate the weight and power behind a tree branch. Even a seemingly small branch can deliver a massive blow, especially if it falls quite a ways, which can lead to injury or sudden death.

Landslides, rockslides, and other slides can also lead to instant injury or death in the bush. If you camp somewhere and there is a sheer rock face, a large rocky mountain, or any other rock formation nearby, you are at risk of that rock formation coming down and burying you, and anyone you are with, under the rocks. Those would also result in instant death. If you were at the top of a terrain that began to slide, you could drop to your death, be struck by something on your way down, or land in water and drown.

You should also beware of wildlife and insects. Wildlife can attack you when you are not paying attention, which can lead to instant death, and certain insects or ground critters can bite you, which can lead to deadly infections. Black widows or brown recluse spiders, for example, can bite, which can lead to your skin dying off, which ultimately turns into a disease that will kill you within hours or days, at best. If you can, keep your bed up and away from the ground, and inspect it before ever getting into it to avoid having any insects or small animals getting into your bedding and harming you. You should also keep the bedding tightly tucked in around you to avoid loose bedding, welcoming dangerous insects into your space.

The best place for your shelter is on dry, flat ground that is naturally sheltered by healthy trees that show no signs of decay or falling down. You can clean away the underbrush from the area to ensure the ground is clear and easy to walk and build on, and less likely to attract bugs and small animals since they prefer dead leaves and other vegetation to hide under. Stay away from large boulders, rock formations, or bodies of water as they can pose a threat to your camp. As well, stay away from common wildlife corridors, marked by frequently used trails, as being too close could result in you attracting dangerous wildlife to your camp.

Short Term Shelter Solutions

If you are surviving for a short period of time, a simple tarp tent with a ground cloth should be plenty to protect you for as long as you need. There are three tarp tents you can make with a tarp, rope, and some rocks or sticks that will help you stake the tarp to the ground. They are easy to make, provide adequate shelter, and are excellent for short term survival situation, including short term overall survival or short term hunting or fishing trips away from your long-term camp. The three tarp tents you can make include a tarp lean-to, a supported flying tarp, or a low lying flying tarp. Each of these shelters can be used for different purposes, and they are all simple to make.

A tarp lean-to can be made by locating four trees that are relatively close together, and that form a square between them. To create your lean-to, you will simply tie each corner of the tarp to the tree, pulling it tight, so it forms a nice taut surface. One half of the tarp should be tied at least one foot higher than the other half. This protects you from rain, as anything that falls on the slanted tarp will immediately fall off rather than leaking, or adding weight to the tarp and eventually causing it to cave in. If you are in an area with any breeze, build the shorter side of the lean-to toward the breeze, so it keeps you protected from the elements.

A supported flying tarp can be made by locating the middle of one of the sides of your tarp and tying it about four to five feet up the trunk of a medium-sized tree. You will then take either corner from the same side that has been tied to the tree and pull it out to a 45-degree angle from the tree and keep it in place using medium to large rocks on the edges of the tarp. The side of the tarp that is opposite the tree should be weighed down by rocks, too. You can tuck the tarp underneath itself and weigh it down with rocks from the inside, as this can prevent precipitation from getting into your shelter.

A low lying flying tarp is made the same way as a supported flying tarp, except that it is far lower to the ground. For a low lying flying tarp, you will tie it only two to three feet up the tree trunk, and you will keep the openings on either side fairly small by folding the corners of the tarp underneath itself and weighing it down from the inside using rocks. You will continue to fold the opposite edge under and weigh it down with rocks, too. This smaller tarp allows for one or two people to sleep snug, prevents wind from being able to get into the tarp, and makes it far less likely that any predators will try to get into your tent and bother you while you are sleeping.

No matter how you position your tarp, you should always clean away the ground underneath the tarp and lay a ground cloth under it. Thick canvas, animal hide, woolen blankets, or other coverings will prevent the cold or damp ground from affecting you while you sleep. You should place these ground cloths even if you have access to a sleeping bag, as they ensure that you are able to stay as warm and protected from the elements as possible.

Long-Term Shelter Solutions

If you are going to need to survive long term, or if you do not have access to a tarp or ground cloths, there are many ways that you can build a shelter out of the resources offered from the land. Branches, leaves, brush, dirt and clay, rocks, and other materials can all be used to form excellent shelters that keep you protected from the elements and offer comfort and security in the wilderness. One excellent element of these shelters, too, is that they are structured out of natural materials, which means that you are better camouflaged into the environment. This way, you are less likely to grab the interest of nearby wildlife and are more likely to remain hidden and left alone when you are in your shelter.

Building a shelter from resources in the forest will vary depending on what you have access to, how big of a shelter you need, and where you are. Rather than attempting to give you specific step-by-step instructions to build various shelters, I will explain how you can improvise and build your own walls, roof, and floor using resources you find in the bush. This way, you know how to improvise and make your own shelter in your own terrain.

Before you build anything for your shelter, clean the ground around where the shelter will be placed. Remove leaves, branches, rocks, and any debris that will interrupt the ground space, as all of this will be too messy for the floor of your shelter. You will want soft, clear space that is less likely to harbor insects or sharp sticks or rocks that could cut your skin or cause bruises or other injuries. In the bush, even minor injuries can become major problems, so you need to avoid them at all costs.

Begin building your shelter with the walls by creating walls that are strong and resistant enough to keep wind and other elements out of your shelter. You will want to build your walls based on the elements you are likely to be exposed to, as minor windy conditions will require much less protection than heavy rainfall or snow. Build your walls based on the worst elements you are most likely to be exposed to so they are adequate for every situation. They also need to be strong enough to hold up the roof you create for your shelter. Your walls should be four-sided like a conventional house. However, there is one type of shelter where they can be adapted, and where they should actually be put on second instead of first. That is, you would build an A-frame roof and build the walls up on the front and back of it. These are great shelters for areas where there is high precipitation or where it is cold, so you want to have a small shelter that does not have a lot of room for wind or other elements to get in. These can also be useful if you are in an area that lacks natural resources such as trees and brush, as they do not require as many materials.

As you build up the walls of your shelter, use larger branches to make the main walls themselves. You can plant the ends in the ground, so they stand up, and then use a rope to tie the branches together if you have any. Then, you can weave small leafy branches, twigs, or pine-covered branches into the larger branches to create insulation and to protect your shelter from the elements. If you have any, extra tarps or ground cloths can also be used to cover the walls; however, the majority of your tarps and ground cloths, if you have them, should be reserved for the roof and floor as these are more important uses for those materials. If you do not have branches to build your walls with, you can build them out of dirt, clay, or snow. Ensure that any shelters made out of these materials are made with thick walls and that they are made in a way where they are unlikely to collapse. Packing down the building materials and giving dirt or clay plenty of time to dry out ensures that they are less likely to collapse.

For your roof, you want to use small to medium branches, and as few as possible. Medium or larger branches could fall through if too much weight were to come on them or if your structure were to be weak somewhere, and those branches could then cause serious injuries. It is better to use long, small to medium branches sparingly to make a basic frame for your roof. Then, you can cover the roof in leafy branches, evergreen branches, grass, large leaves, or anything else you can find that will create a nice thick cover. Be sure to use a few layers of your roof materials to build your roof, as this ensures that precipitation and weather elements cannot penetrate your roof and cause you to get wet inside. As well, ensure you do not let the roof get too heavy as this will lead to it collapsing and possibly causing an injury. Always make your roof in an A-frame shape, or in a lean-to shape with one side shorter than the other, as this will allow precipitation to naturally fall off and will prevent any damaged parts of your roof from falling directly on you. If you have a spare tarp, you can use, place a tarp over the roof frame but under the natural materials, as this will provide an added layer of protection from the weather, without attracting attention to your shelter.

Lastly, you need to build the floor. The floor should be built at the end because this way, you can quickly go through and sweep out any building materials that may have fallen into your floor when you were building your shelter. Once you have cleaned out the floor of your shelter, you need to insulate it, too. In the wilderness, the ground holds a lot of moisture, even if you have built a shelter over it. Covering the ground with dry materials ensures that you are not exposed to that moisture. In addition to moisture, the ground can become quite cold, which can lead to your body temperature dropping. Proper insulation in your shelter can prevent this. The best materials to use to insulate your floor are soft brush, such as small branches covered in leaves or evergreen branches. Shake them out to eliminate bugs, and then lay your ground cloth over them if you have one to keep yourself insulated. If you are going to be surviving for extended periods of time, you can also dry and cure any pelts you get from animals you trap or hunt, and then layer those pelts over the floor of your shelter. Excess can also be layered over the walls and on the ceiling of your shelter, as the more you have, the warmer your shelter will be. Again, be cautious not to place too much on your roof or hang too much from your ceiling, as this can cause it to collapse, and that could cause injury or worse.

CHAPTER 7

The Third Essential: Fire

After you have your water and shelter figured out, you need fire. Fire is an essential element to survival as it allows you to maintain a proper core body temperature, allows you to cook your foods to safe eating temperatures, and provides you with the opportunity to sterilize things. In the wilderness, smoke baths are a great way to cleanse yourself and sterilize yourself of any bacteria, as smoke is known for creating an acidic environment and eliminating harsh bacteria. Fire provides an abundance of benefits in the bush, so long as you have built the right fire for the purpose you require because, like anything, fire is a tool for survival.

For short term survival situations, you should be able to use your fire-starting materials that you brought with you. Your lighter is good to start your fire, and you can forage for wood in the forest around so that you have fuel for it. Brush like leaves, evergreen branches, and even some brambles are excellent for keeping small fires going for short survival experiences.

If you are in a long-term survival situation, you will need to have more supplies on hand to help you with your fire. Building up a stock of cut wood and giving it time to dry out, and keeping plenty of kindling and fire starter on hand will be important. You should also know how to use a magnifying glass to start a fire, as well as have a ferrocerium rod, or a flint rod, which can start fires without the need for matches or lighters. This way, you have everything you need to start as many fires as are required.

Where to Build Your Fire

There are a few different areas where you will build a fire during a survival situation. In short term survival situations, building a fire directly in your camp, about three feet away from your shelter, is plenty to keep you warm and dry. A fire should be built in this same location if you are staying long-term. However, this will be the only fire that you will need in a short term situation. Any situation that will last longer than 24 hours, or where you will need to actually cook over your open fire, will require you to have a fire built elsewhere, too.

Food fires should always be built at least 100 yards away from your shelter, so that as you cook your food, you are not attracting predators to your actual camp. Understand that even after the fire is out and everything has been cleaned, the smell of cooked food will linger on everything that was around or has come into contact with that fire or any tools used to cook food over or around that fire. In fact, this is why you should also have separate clothes that you use for cooking, and they should be stored away from your shelter, too.

Another place where you may want to build a fire would be if you were away from camp hunting or fishing and needed to build a fire for warmth, water purification, or cooking food on the go. These fires are usually much smaller, require fewer materials, so they are easier to start and maintain. Aside from these three areas, you should not require any further fires in your survival experience.

Building a Birds Nest

The first step for building any fire is to have adequate fire-starting materials. Many fire starter materials can be collected from home, while others can be gathered from the bush. In the bush, things like pine needles, dry moss, and dry grass or brush can be used to start a fire.

From home, the fire starter materials you can bring include:

- Crumpled or shredded paper
- Cotton balls
- Tampons
- Cotton, linen, and other plant-based material
- Dryer lint
- Wood shavings
- Greasy chips
- Cardboard
- Pinecones
- Wax from candles

A great way to create fire starters is to take a cardboard toilet paper roll and cut it into 3 sections. Then, fill the center of the toilet paper roll with dryer lint, cotton balls, or scraps of plant-based materials. Cover the entire thing in candle wax to keep it all sealed together and then store it in a plastic bag so it does not get wet. You can make as many of these as possible and bring them all with you for starting your fires with.

If you do not have fire-starting materials from home, the bush has plenty to offer. The most common way to make a fire starter in the wilderness is to make what survivalists call a "birds nest." Birds' nests are made in pretty much the same way a bird would actually make their nest. You will take twigs and scraps of vegetation off of the ground and weave it together into a bird's nest shape. The shape allows for plenty of oxygen to move through the starting materials, while also keeping them close enough together that the fire can reasonably spread through the materials.

Once you have made the bird's nest, it will be placed in your fire so you can start the fire itself. Despite the fact that the bird's nest is responsible for starting the fire, it should be the last thing you place in your fire as you want to keep it safe from being damaged in case one of your fire logs falls on it. Instead, you will start by clearing space on the ground for you to place your fire, and then you will surround the fire with rocks so that it does not travel and cause a major fire in the bush. Next, you will build your log formation in the fire pit. Then, you will place the bird's nest in the log formation and start that on fire. This will then catch fire and eventually catch your logs on fire, giving you a steady, strong fire that can be maintained for long periods of time.

Just like with the initial log formation, the starter and log formation themselves do not need to be maintained after the fire is started. It is perfectly fine that the bird's nest completely burns away and that the logs fall out of formation as they burn away. Simply place new logs over the fire in a way that prevents them from smothering the fire, so plenty of oxygen can get in and help the fire spread to the new logs. This way, your fire can last for as long as you need it to.

Fire for Heat

Fire that is created for keeping you warm needs to be made in a way where you can easily sit around it, and where you can trust that it will be long-lasting. If you are trying to keep warm outside of your shelter, you want your fire to be no more than three feet tall, but no less than about one and a half feet tall. Any taller than three feet and your fire runs the risk of catching the forest itself on fire, while anything smaller than one and a half feet can run the risk of it burning out and leading to you getting cold. Overnight, you want a proper fire that can last for hours without going out so that as you sleep, you can stay warm. The only time this may not be true is if you are surviving in an area where the temperatures do not drop any lower than about 15 degrees, as you can use your sleeping bag to keep you warm and comfortable during the night. Anything lower, though, and you will need a long-lasting fire for heat.

For daytime, the best fire lays for heat include the teepee fire lay, the lean-to fire lay, or the log cabin fire lay. The long-burning fire lay and the Dakota fire pit are also excellent for keeping you warm, with the long-burning fire working overnight, and the Dakota fire pit keeping you warm during windy conditions.

Teepee Fire Lay

The teepee fire lay is the most common fire lay that people think of. It is frequently taught in scouts and other survival programs, and it offers excellent fire for warmth. This fire lay is not good for cooking because it is too tall, it gets too hot, and it does not offer a reliable location for cooking your food over.

To build the teepee fire lay, prepare your fire location by clearing the ground and outlining the fire pit with rocks. Then, start by taking kindling-size branches that are about 1 foot long each and build a teepee shape with them, crossing them at the top ends to keep them in place. If you can, find a piece of kindling with a "Y" shape at the end and use that as your starting point. Make sure you keep the kindling far enough apart that plenty of oxygen can get through.

Once you have built a teepee out of kindling, you will need to build a teepee out of branches, or fuel logs. Again, keep these branches far enough apart that oxygen can get through easily, as oxygen is essential to your fire being able to start and thrive.

Finally, place your bird's nest in the center of the kindling teepee and light it on fire. It will burn, catch the kindling on fire, and then the kindling will catch your fuel logs on fire. Add fresh fuel logs one at a time to keep the fire going, and add them carefully to avoid smothering the fire you have already started.

Lean-to Fire Lay

A lean-to fire lay is an excellent fire lay that is easy to build, that offers plenty of oxygen for your fire to grow, and that makes it extremely easy for you to get your starter in the bottom of your fire lay. To build a lean-to fire, you need to clear your space for your fire to be placed, then you need to place one larger log on an angle, propped up against kindling or a small rock. Next, you will layer larger kindling or small fuel logs over that leaning branch. You will lean the ends up around them, creating a half-circle of logs in such a way that they look like a small shelter or a lean-to. Your lean-to should get shorter and smaller on the end near the ground, and longer or taller on the end at the top of the propped-up stick.

Once you have set up your lean-to fire lay, you can place your bird's nest in the opening made from the propped up log. Then, you will light the bird's nest on fire. It will catch your kindling pieces on fire, and then the larger fuel log that is holding the fire lay in place. As you place logs over the fire, be careful not to smother them.

Log Cabin Fire Lay

A log cabin fire lay is a simple crisscross style fire lay that has a teepee shape built inside of it. Your log cabin fire lay is not particularly tall, but it does offer plenty of fuel to keep it going for long periods of time. A well-built log cabin fire lay should last several hours, at least. While it is not enough for an overnight fire, it will get you plenty of warmth.

To create a log cabin fire lay, you will start by sourcing several pieces of kindling, and then approximately 10 pieces of fuel logs that are about one and a half to two feet long. You will first make a teepee shape with kindling in the center of your cleaned fire pit that has been sectioned off with larger rocks. Then, you will lay two of your fuel logs beside your fire, on opposite sides, running lengthwise across the fire pit. Next, you will stack two of your fuel fire logs across the edges of the two you originally laid, creating a square-shape with the logs now. Lay two logs over the same direction as your original two logs, then two crisscross over those. Lay two more logs in the same direction as your original two logs. You should have 10 logs in a log cabin shape around your teepee, and a well-built teepee in the middle.

Now, all you need to do is place your bird's nest in the center of the teepee and light it on fire. The fire will catch the kindling, then eventually, the kindling will catch the log cabin shape, and it will start to burn. Because of the formation, it should last several hours if you used large enough fuel logs.

Long Burning Fire Lay

A long burning fire lay is excellent for keeping you warm all night long. It is achieved by digging out a long pit, filling it with fuel logs, and burning it from one end to the other. The idea is that you start a slow fire with a controlled amount of oxygen, and the result is the fire burns all night long. To create a long burning fire lay for yourself, you will start by digging a narrow ditch about 6 feet long. It should be wide enough to hold logs, and long enough that it runs at least the length of your body.

Once you have dug the ditch, you want to source fuel logs that can be placed along the ditch itself. Make sure they reach from one end to the other, so you have a six foot length of logs that will be burnt overnight. Leave about a foot of space at the end of the ditch without any fuel logs, and create a teepee fire lay in that space using smaller kindling, and then larger kindling. Then, place your bird's nest in the teepee formation and light it on fire. As it burns, ensure that the edge of your first fuel log is placed close enough that it catches on fire from your kindling fire. Once it catches, you can trust that the entire six foot log fire will burn throughout the night, keeping you warm while you sleep.

Dakota Fire Pit

Dakota fire pits are excellent for inconspicuous fires, or fires built in windy areas. The way the pit is built, the fire remains relatively unseen and unaffected by elements like wind. These firepits are also excellent for cooking over, as you can make the surface area of the fire rather small, and it is level with the ground, which means you can place a pan over it and allow it to cook using the heat from your fire.

To create a Dakota fire pit, you will start by sourcing small pieces of kindling. You want a large amount, as it is unlikely that you will be creating a large fire pit for your fire. If you were to create your fire pit too large, it would defeat the purpose, and the wind would still pose a threat to your fire. Instead, you want to dig a pit about 1 foot across and 1.5 feet deep. Then, you will move about 2 feet away from the pit you have dug and dig another pit at an angle, aiming toward the bottom of your original pit. Once you are about to connect the two, use your hand to dig away any dirt that remains between your two pits so you can connect them without collapsing the dirt above your newly formed tunnel. It is important that your tunnel is at least as thick as your arm, if not a little larger, as this is where your fire will receive the oxygen it needs to thrive. Without this oxygen tunnel, your fire pit would lack oxygen, and your fire would burn out.

Once your pit and tunnel are properly built, you can go ahead and build a teepee fire shape in the main pit. Add your bird's nest into the bottom of the teepee and light it on fire. If you need to, you can reach your arm through the oxygen tunnel and light the bird's nest on fire this way to avoid burning yourself. You can continue adding smaller pieces of wood into your pit as needed, as the oxygen tunnel will continue to fuel your fire with enough oxygen each time you add a new log. Simply make sure you do not add such a thick log that the entire main pit is filled, as you will still fail to get enough oxygen into your fire if you do this.

Fire for Cooking

The Dakota fire pit is an excellent all-around fire for warmth and cooking. There are two additional fire lays you can use, however, which will also help you with cooking food at your camp. Note that while you could technically cook over any fire, safely placing your cookware over the fires would be challenging, and the size of the fires would result in your cookware becoming too hot and you instantly burning anything you attempted to cook. Cooking fires should be small and easy to contain, and they should burn hot yet slow, as you will not be cooking over the flame itself but rather over the embers at the bottom of the fire. This ensures that your food will be cooked all the way through without becoming burnt from the flames, and you will remain healthy.

Pyramid Fire Lay

The pyramid fire lay is similar to the log cabin one, except that instead of creating a teepee in the center and a log cabin around it, you will be using the same method of interlocking the logs and turning kindling-sized pieces of wood into a pyramid shape. To make your pyramid fire lay, look for several uniformed pieces of kindling that you can stack together to make your pyramid.

Once you have found your pieces, lay two pieces of kindling on the ground parallel to each other. Then, lay two parallel pieces in the opposite direction, over the edges of the original two pieces you laid down. Keep doing this, going back and forth in either direction, and moving the kindling closer and closer together until it comes together in the center, but leave a small gap open in the top. About halfway through, add a bird's nest into the bottom and make sure you leave gaps large enough that will let you catch the bird's nest starter on fire.

As soon as the fire lay is set up, you can light your bird's nest on fire and let the fire catch. The pyramid should burn down quickly, yet it is easy for you to keep it going as long as you need to in order to keep the embers hot. If the pyramid burns too low,

Star Fire With a Cooking Arm

A star fire with a cooking arm is a more advanced contraption, but it can still be made from the bush. To make your star fire with a cooking arm, you will start with the fire lay. The star fire lay requires you to have at least 4 fuel sized pieces of wood, though more is always better. You will bring one point from each piece of wood together in the center and evenly space the opposite points out around the center, making a star shape. Under the center of your star, you should dig out a small depression so that your fire has plenty of oxygen to keep it burning. You should also leave slight gaps between the ends of the logs, as this allows even more oxygen to flow through and keep your fire thriving.

In the center of your fire lay, you should keep the points separated by about a foot, so they create a circle but are not all touching in the very middle. Then, you will lay a bird's nest in the center and cover it loosely with some kindling.

Before you light your fire, you will want to find a large, sturdy Y-shaped branch and bury the single end down in the ground at least one foot. You can also stack rocks around it to prevent it from falling. You should place this stick about 2-3 feet away from your fire lay, facing toward the fire so that when you balance a branch between it, the branch points toward the center of your fire. The top of the Y-shape should be only about 3-4 feet high, as this will ensure that it is not too high for you to cook with. The branch itself should be thick enough that if you placed a loaded Dutch oven on it, it would not bend or break. Then, you want to find another large, but not too thick, branch that can be placed through the Y-shape, with one end up above the fire. If you can, bury the end of the single branch that will be hanging over the fire, or cover it with heavy rocks and other items that will prevent it from falling once you anchor a Dutch oven to the opposite end.

Now, start your fire by lighting the bird's nest and letting the kindling get going. Then, once it is going well, you can load up your Dutch oven or a steel pot and hang it on the branch itself. The fire should not be touching the bottom of the pot, but it should be high enough that the bottom of the pot is receiving consistent, high temperatures that will cook the contents inside of the pot. Be sure to use heavy duty cooking gloves or another branch to remove your pot from over the fire, as it will be extremely hot when you are done cooking with it.

CHAPTER 8

The Fourth Essential: Food

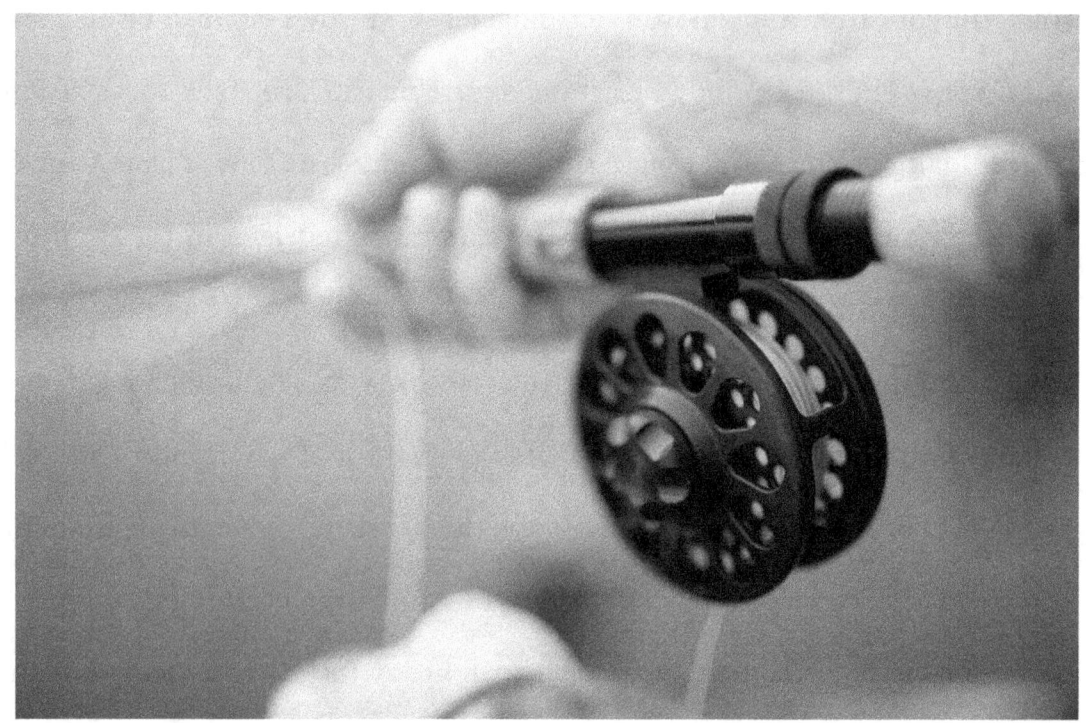

While you can last three weeks without food, the reality is that the energy it takes to survive in the bush is far greater than it takes to survive in an urban environment. Even if you are in an urban environment but have been cut off from your usual sources, you will find yourself burning a lot more energy to maintain your livelihood, which results in you burning more energy and needing more calories. Anytime you put excess demand on your body this way, it is essential to stock up on calories as quickly as possible to make up for the deficit. Otherwise, you could start seeing the negative symptoms of hunger caused by not eating. While it may take you three weeks to die of starvation, it only takes on average a few hours to start feeling the adverse side effects of not eating, and three to five days to start feeling wholly drained due to the lack of calories.

Eating in the bush can seem intimidating because you have to make sure that anything you are eating is safe to consume. Foraging for vegetation, catching fish, and trapping or hunting wildlife are all of the ways you will gain food, but if you do it wrong in any way, you could find yourself facing a nasty infection or parasite that could deteriorate your health, and fast. Fortunately, there are many steps you can take to ensure that eating in the bush will be safe and that you will remain healthy from the food you have consumed. As far as timelines go, you should aim to find food to consume within the first twenty-four hours of being on-site. If you need to, you can start with foraging for food as this is an excellent way to get the food you need quickly, and you do not have to rely on wildlife to take the bait and land in your trap or on your hook. Once you have done that, though, you need to start looking for animal protein as it will have all of the calories and nutrients that you need to keep your body going during those days where you are challenging your body more than usual.

Types of Food to Eat in the Wilderness

In the wilderness there are five types of food you can consume, four of which are considered an animal protein. The first type of food you can consume in the wilderness is foraged vegetation, including berries, herbs, vegetables, and other plants that are safe for human consumption. These are important as they provide you with an abundance of vitamins, which ensures that you have all of the vitamins and minerals that you need to thrive.

The four types of animal protein you can consume in the wilderness include fish, reptiles, birds, and small to medium mammals. While you could technically aim to hunt and destroy a more massive mammal unless you have adequate means for preserving that meat before it spoils, it is not generally a good idea. You could find yourself wasting the meat and attracting far too many predators to your camp.

Foraging for Vegetation

Foraging for vegetation is something that cannot be summarized in one single beginner's guide dedicated to survival as a whole. This particular topic contains so many nuances that are unique to your geographic area. The best way to safely forage for vegetation is to have a proper wildcrafting or foraging book that reflects your unique geographical region and to have that in your G'n'G bag so that you can bring it with you if you ever find yourself in a survivalist situation. If you want to be even safer, you can consider hiring a local herbalist or wildcrafter who is skilled with the local flora and who can show you what to look for and what to avoid. Nearly every plant has poisonous lookalikes that can lead to anything from minor illness or injury to severe illness or even death. It is imperative that you learn how to tell these plants apart, as this ensures you know how to safely forage from the forest without accidentally gathering something that could poison yourself and your entire camp. In short term survival situations, you may be able to survive without forage, but anything more than a few days should involve forage as you will need the extra vitamins and minerals from plants to avoid putting yourself at risk of malnutrition-related illness.

Once you have foraged, you will need to clean your vegetation for safe consumption and store it properly. Soak your harvest in already-filtered water for at least thirty minutes to eliminate unwanted bacteria and debris from it, then run the vegetation through additional filtered water so that you can remove anything off of the surface of your foraged goods. If you want to cook it into a meal, you can do that, too. Some vegetation is only safe to eat once it has been prepared, so be sure you are aware of the consumption rules around different flora before consuming it.

To store your vegetation, you want to use a breathable bag that you can seal to prevent insects or small animals from getting into your foraged food and consuming it or introducing unwanted bacteria to your harvested matter. While it is usually easy to access more vegetation, you do not want to expend any more energy than you need to, so if you are able to collect a fair amount of it at once, you will want to preserve it for a few days of eating.

One thing I do want to be sure you are aware of is the importance of ethical foraging. When foraging, even for a survival situation, it is imperative that you refrain from harvesting an entire crop of anything. Even if you believe there are many more crops in the forest, it is important that you never take more than about 10% of what is available. Over-harvesting can lead to those crops becoming depleted, and if you do find yourself in a long-term situation, it can lead to you not having enough to consume at later dates.

Further, even small instances of over-harvesting can disrupt the harmony of the forest and lead to long-term damage.

Hunting, Trapping, and Fishing

Hunting, trapping, and fishing are the three ways that you will get animal protein into your stomach in the woods. Trapping and fishing are usually the easiest, since hunting would require some form of weapon, and unless you already have weapons with you, it is challenging to make a homemade weapon strong enough to humanely kill a mammal without causing a large amount of suffering beforehand.

All trapping is accomplished using a snare, though the way the snare is set up will often differ depending on what you are trying to trap, and where you are setting the snare up. There are two important snare setups that you need to know about when it comes to trapping animals in the wilderness, which will ensure that you are successful in your endeavors. The first is a squirrel snare, and the second is a snare that will capture just about any other type of animal.

A squirrel snare is a series of traps created along a branch. To create one, you will start by finding a reasonably long branch that you can prop up against a tree, reaching to the lower branches of the tree you have propped your branch up on. Squirrels, by nature, will use this branch to get to the ground. Once you have your branch, you will take your snare line, twist a loop into one end of it, and feed the opposite end through your loop so that you have a slip knot. Then, you will fix the snare to the branch in a way that holds it open so that as the squirrel runs down the branch, they will be caught in the snare and effectively trapped. You should set multiple snares on a single branch to maximize your ability to catch squirrels.

A regular snare can be set by making another slip knot with your snare line. To do so, twist a loop into one end of your snare line and feed the opposite end through the loop, so you have a slip knot. Then, you need to look for animal highways or corridors. These usually look like well-worn paths that indicate that animals frequently use that particular area. Once you have found an animal highway or corridor, you want to follow a smaller worn-in trail that leads into the brush, as this indicates that it is routinely used by small to medium animals. Then, you want to fix the free line of your trap to a branch and set the snare so that it sits open over the path itself. This way, when a small mammal or bird runs down the trail, they will get caught in the snare line and die.

Anytime you set a snare, wear plastic over your hands, either using gloves or a garbage bag or wash your hands with dirt and charcoal to remove your scent. Humans do emit pheromones that animals can smell, and the second they pick up on your pheromones, they will stay far away from your snares, which will lead to failed trapping endeavors. If you do not have anything available, start a small fire about 50 yards away from your trapping site and let it burn long enough that you can harvest charcoal from it and use that. As it burns, stand directly in the smoke for a few minutes to help eliminate your scent from your clothes and the rest of your body, too.

If after a few days, your snares are not catching anything, you may need to adjust their location or set a piece of bait on the other side of the snare that will encourage an animal to reach through it. Be sure to use a form of bait that is nice and smelly, and that is made up of some sort of food item that is not easy to find in your area. For example, if you wanted to catch a small rodent, you might use sardine oil or something similar as a bait to encourage them to go through the trap. This way, the animal has more incentive, and your traps are more likely to catch a harvest.

Fishing is just as easy as trapping, if not easier. All you need to do is find a river, creek, or lake that has a nice deep pit in it where the water is not moving too quickly. Then, you want to tie a piece of fishing line around a branch that is around four to five feet long and two inches thick. Avoid thin branches, as they will snap under the weight of a fish.
When you have the right sized branch, tie a fishing line on one end with a hook on the end of it. Attach some bait to the hook, which can be anything from a small insect to a piece of raw game meat. Drop your baited line into the water and keep it slowly moving, so it behaves like live bait, which will encourage the fish to bite. It may take up to half an hour or even an hour to catch a fish, though if you wait any longer than that, it may mean that you are not in an optimal fishing location and need to search for somewhere better to catch your fish from.

Butchering Small to Medium Game

Once you have caught your animal, you need to know how to butcher it. Small to medium game is all butchered roughly the same, as their physical bodies are usually quite similar. For example, a rabbit, a rat, a squirrel, and a raccoon would all have similar body shapes and organ placements, meaning the butchering process would be more or less the same.

To butcher your small to medium game, you will start by hanging their back legs from a branch that would place the animal at a height that was easy to work with. Place a pot or some form of contraption under the animal so you can catch all of the blood and unwanted pieces of the animal, as this will help you hide your scent trail later. If you are butchering a squirrel or something of similar size, you can skip the hanging process and just hold the animal upside down over a small bowl. Once you have the animal placed, you will use a sharp knife to slit their throats so that they can bleed out. If your animal is small enough, you can remove the head all at once. If not, wait until it bleeds out and then cut the rest of the head off.

Once the animal has bled out, you will remove the pelt. For small game, you can do this by cutting off all of their feet and their head and then cutting from the inside of one back leg across to the inside of another back leg, so the pelt is separated and then pulling it down toward the head until it is removed. For a medium game, use a sharp knife and cut around the back ankles. Then, cut from one of the ankles to the opposite ankle, running your blade above the tail, so you do not cut into the genital area. Cut off the front feet and the head and tug the pelt down over the head. If your pelt is large enough to be used, cut up one side of it, so it is one flat piece or cut both sides, so you have two parts, and then hang it out to dry by attaching one rope to each corner of the pelt and hanging it, so the pelt is taut.

After the pelt is removed, you will go to the belly side of the animal and make a small incision where their belly button would be, taking caution not to cut into their organs. If you cut into their organs, bile or other digestive enzymes can leach into your meat and render it inedible, so be very careful. Once you have cut a small slit in the belly button, insert your finger and press the organs back, then carefully cut from that slit all the way down to the chest cavity, so you have a large opening over their belly. Next, you will reach into that opening and carefully use your hands to break all of the connective tissues and pull the organs out in front of the animal. Once everything is disconnected and hanging out, you will cut around the genitals to completely remove the intestines from the animal. Throw them away, unless you want to keep the heart and liver, in which case harvest those first and then throw the rest away.

Once your animal has been cut and entrails removed, you can start cutting your pieces. Start by cutting off the front legs and placing them in your consumption container. Then, cut along the spine on either side and remove the flank meat. Lastly, remove meat from the breast area if you have an animal that contained a large amount of breast meat. Then, cut off the back legs and remove the feet if you have not already.

You can also leave your animal intact, not removing any segments of the meat, if you plan on cooking it whole. For animals like squirrels and rabbits, this is perfectly fine as you should have an easy enough time cooking them thoroughly over your fire. For hares or larger animals, however, it is recommended that you cut them down so you can cook them evenly and thoroughly and avoid getting sick from undercooked meat.

Butchering Birds

Butchering birds is different from mammals since they have two legs and wings, and their organs are placed differently than they are for mammals. To butcher a bird, you will need a flat, clean work surface. If you have a table, use that. If not, lay a clean tarp out over a flat spot on the ground and do your butchering there.

You will start the process by first boiling a large pot of water, big enough that you can submerge the entire bird in. As the water warms up, cut the birds head off and let it bleed out into your discard bucket. Then, once the water is warm enough and the bird is bled out, you can hold it by the foot and dip it into the boiling pot of water and move it around. After about 30 seconds, remove the bird and try to pull a feather off of the wing. Keep submerging the bird for about 15 seconds at a time until the wing feathers easily pull off. Once they do, stop submerging the bird and pluck all of the feathers off.

Next, lay the bird on your flat work surface and cut their feet off at the knees. Use your sharp knife to cut the cartilage in the knees, then use your hands to pry the joint apart. Do not use your knife on bones as you will dull it out, and then you will have to sharpen it before you can finish the process. For small birds like doves or quails, you can remove their wings as they are too small to consume. For larger birds like ducks or geese, you can leave them on if you wish.

Once the feet and wings are removed, you will need to remove the neck and gizzards, and then the guts from your bird. Start with the neck. To do so, take your knife and cut around the entire neck area, being careful not to cut into any of the innards. Then, reach in with your hand and remove the innards from your bird. If you are not going to eat the neck and gizzard, throw them into your discard bucket. Next, go to the vent side of the bird, locate the breast bone, and make an incision a few inches below that. Cut carefully around the vent until you reach the tail, and then reach your hands into the incision you have made and gently pull apart all of the connective tissues that hold the organs in place. Pull the organs out as you go, so they are on the outside of your bird. Once you have all of the entrails removed, you can lift them up out of the way and cut beneath the tail, again taking care not to damage any of the organs as you do. At that point, the organs should easily fall out of your bird.

Butchering Fish and Reptiles

Butchering fish and reptiles is different from game and birds because their organs are wildly different from mammals. They are still incredibly easy to butcher, though, and they offer excellent protein when needed.

For fish, you will start by running the back of your knife over your fish to descale it. After you have descaled the fish, cut off the head and tail, and then the fins. Then, take your blade and place it just above the midline of the stomach, by the tail end. Insert your blade most of the way into the fish, but not all the way up through the top spinal area, and slice all the way to the front of the fish. Do this again on the bottom of the midline of the stomach. Once you are done, reach in and pull the midline out, and with it, all of the guts should come out, too. If you have a female fish, the eggs should also be easy to remove at this point, also. You can cook or preserve the fish this way, or when you are ready to cook the fish, you could cut it all the way in half and remove the bones then cook it over your fire.

For reptiles, it depends on what type of reptile you are butchering. Snakes can be slaughtered by cutting off their heads and tails, then descaling and slicing them similar to how you would with a fish, before removing their entrails. For reptiles or amphibians with legs, like lizards or frogs, the process is slightly different. Both lizards and frogs have strong skin, so you will first remove their head and all four feet. Then, you will make an incision into their stomach, cutting through the thick skin. This will take some force, but be careful not to cut too hard, or you will damage the organs, and render the meat useless. Once you have made the incision, you will cut all the way around until you have one large incision around the midsection of the animal. Then, you will tug the skin off the top and bottom, leaving you with a skinned reptile or amphibian. At this point, you can easily remove all of the organs by carefully tugging off the connective tissues and letting the organs fall out of the stomach area, before cutting them away. What's left should be only the edible meat portions of your reptile or amphibian. Because they are so small, there is no need to cut them into sections.

Cleaning and Cooking Wild-Caught Meat

As soon as you are done butchering any sort of wild-caught meat, whether it is a small mammal, bird, fish, or reptile, you need to clean it. Clean your meat by pouring fresh, filtered water over it and ensuring that all of the excess blood, veins, and other little debris are washed away from your meat. Then, get your meat cool as soon as possible. If you have cool water, you can drop your meat into that; if not, you can place it in a tarp and tie it up then float it in a stream of cool water. You want the meat to cool down as soon as possible, so it does not spoil.

When you are ready to cook your meat, you will either place it in a piece of cookware or attach it to a large branch using some form of wire or twine and then you will place it in the low part of the fire, just above the embers. Cook your meat until it is charred on the outside and until it appears overcooked on the inside. It may not taste as good this way, but this will prevent you from accidentally ingesting undercooked meat, which could lead to illness, parasitic infection, or other issues, all of which could be fatal in the bush.

Properly Storing Food

Any food you cannot immediately consume needs to be properly stored. If you are in a snowy area, store leftover food in containers by digging a hole into the snow, burying them, and then marking where they have been buried so you can locate them later on. One way you can store your meat if you do not have snow is by drying it. Slice the meat thin and hang it over fire smoke until it is completely dried out, or let it sit in direct sunlight until it is completely dried out. In this case, you need to cut the meat as thin as possible so you can dry it out quickly, as it could become contaminated if it takes too long. Smoke will both dry the meat out and kill off any bacteria, as smoke is acidic and can protect the meat itself.

Another way to store your meat is to salt it. To do this, you want to coat the meat in salt and then store it in a container. Salt makes the outsides of the meat undesirable to bacteria, as it turns them acidic. You will still need to cook the meat even if you have salt cured it.

Once you have properly cured your meat, you need to place it and your vegetation matter into some form of a bag. You can use a bag you already have, or you can lay everything in the center of a tarp and tie the edges together, so it forms a bag around your food. Then, to safely store your food, you need to hang it from a tree. Hanging your food ensures that no one can get to it, so long as you do it properly. Any other method of storage, such as hiding it or burying it, would lead to your food being dug up and taken by a predator, and it could lead to your cooking camp becoming a dangerous location as predators may come back in search of more.

To hang your food from a tree, you want to find a branch that is high enough that an animal could not reach it from below or above. Understand that large bears can reach as high as six feet, so you need to have your food anchored quite high above the ground. It should also not be anchored anywhere near your camp, or your cooking camp. Keep it at least 100 yards away from your sleeping camp, and 50 yards away from your cooking camp. To anchor it, start by taking a small stick that is around 4 inches long and 2 inches wide and tying a piece of rope around it. This is called a "toggle." Then, toss that over your chosen branch that will be able to keep your food safest. Tie the other end of your rope around the food bag, then simply pull until the food bag is suspended high in the air, but not close to any branches or to the tree trunk of the tree it is hanging from, or any other tree trunk. It should primarily be hanging over a clearing. Then, take the end with the toggle and tie it around the tree, using the toggle to tie it tight and keep it well-fastened in place. Your food should now be safe until you are ready to obtain it for consumption later on. Anytime you come back for your food, be particularly aware of any predators, as the fact that they cannot access your food does not mean that they will not be attracted to the area. They may linger around, trying to look for a way to access it, so you need to be extra cautious to avoid accidentally walking up on a hungry predator.

Long-Term Gardening Solutions

If you are in the wilderness for an extended period of time, you need to start learning how to garden. Long-term gardening solutions ensure that you have a plentiful supply of fresh produce for as long as you need it. Gardening can be done by foraging for seeds from local flora, or you can pack seeds of the hardiest plants for your survival area's hardiness zone in your G'n'G bag for just in case. If you do this, be sure to update your seeds from time to time as they will go dormant and die eventually if they are not used.

The best way to engage in a long-term gardening solution in the wilderness is to build raised bed gardens and forage for soil from the local area to fill your raised bed gardens with. Large branches off of trees can easily be used to build your gardens, as can larger rocks. Once your bed is filled, you can place your seeds in it and tend to it as you would with a regular garden. The benefit here is that you have access to a consistent crop and that you can consume food without having to go searching for it all the time. However, you will need to be cautious as omnivores and herbivores like deer, mice, rabbits, and other animals may find your garden and start eating it. While this may seem like a great way to get your hands on more animal protein, it is also a great way to lose access to your abundant garden. You may need to build some form of fence or protection to keep your garden safe so no one can steal it from you.

CHAPTER 9

The Fifth Essential: Safety

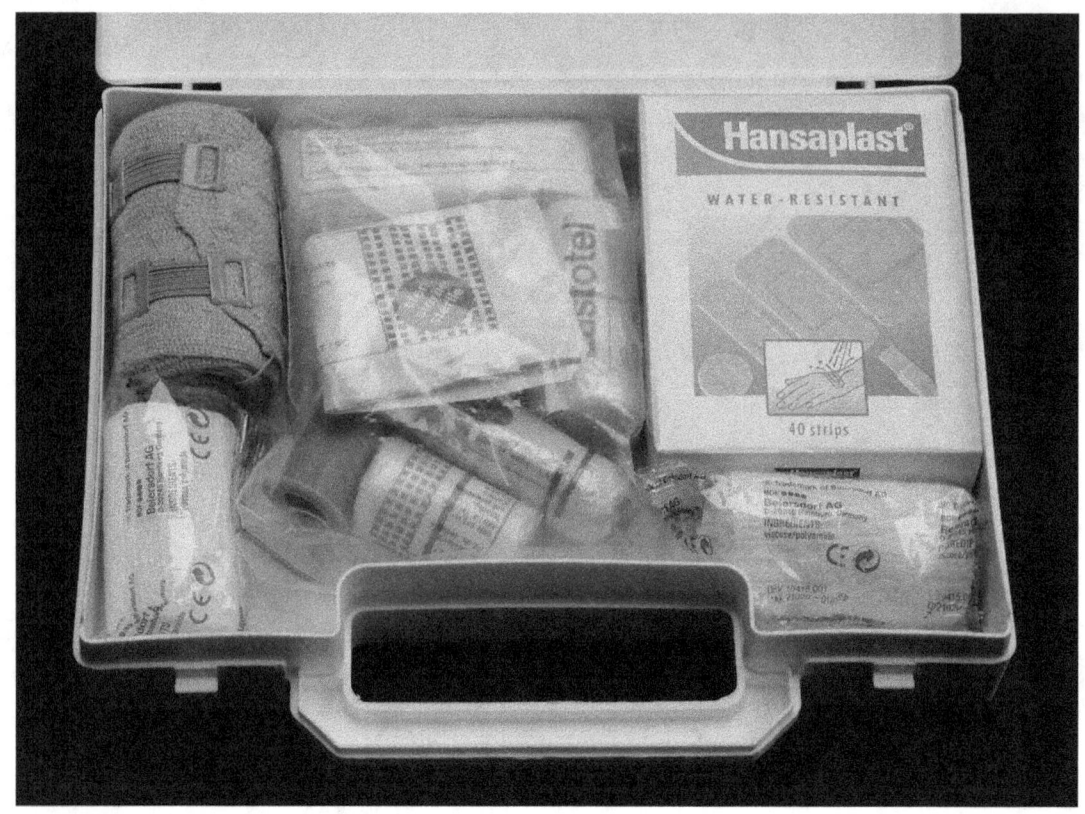

Safety is an essential part of survival, as unsafe conditions can lead to accidental illness, injury, or death. Your mental, emotional, and physical health are all at risk when you are unable to maintain your safety, as you will find yourself living in constant fear and likely being harmed by the dangers around you. The better you protect yourself, the longer you can survive. It is essential that you cover all safety bases, and that you do not take any for granted, as a lack of safety in any area of your life can lead to serious side effects.

At home, practicing safety seems standard and is often considered a form of common sense. For example, don't touch a hot stove, never leave a gas burner on unattended, or don't fall asleep in the bathtub. In the bush, safety can be far more challenging to navigate because you are not entirely aware of what the dangers are or how they could affect you. Another aspect of safety that many people do not realize is how much easier it is to get sick in the bush. At home, your environment is usually sterile, and if it isn't, you have immediate access to first aid equipment or a doctor if one is needed. This means that if you get sick or injured, you have a sterile environment to get better in, or if you need access to medical care you have a trained professional to help you.

There are many more risks in the wilderness you may not be aware of, as well as far fewer sterilization guidelines and medical experts who can help you navigate sickness or injury. Learning how to keep your environment as clean as possible, practice essential hygiene steps to keep yourself clean and safe, and know how to handle first aid situations, so you are less likely to find yourself in a dangerous situation. This way, if anything does go wrong, you know how to navigate it, and you can navigate it quickly.

Rather than attempting to rely on the common sense that keeps you safe in an urban environment, it is critical that you educate yourself on the real harms of the wilderness and how you can protect yourself from those harms. The more you can protect yourself, the better.

Protecting Yourself From Predators

The first and possibly most obvious safety risk you need to be aware of in the bush is predators. Aside from the already-known widowmakers, predators are also an issue. Predators are often viewed as being large, obviously aggressive mammals such as bears, wolves, or other animals that are routinely depicted in movies as the dangers of the wilderness. The reality is, there are far more predators in the wilderness than you are likely aware of. Foxes, coyotes, bobcats, lynx, cougars, and other large animals are all considered predators. Even smaller mammals like badgers, wolverines, and Tasmanian devils are all wildly dangerous and can cause harm to you. If you come across a moose, a buck, or any male species of animal that has horns such as elk, antelope, mountain goats, or otherwise, you may also be at risk. Especially during mating season, these animals can be quite dangerous and will use their antlers or horns to attack you, and they can cause fatal injuries in minimal timing.

From the ground, venomous spiders, bugs, and reptiles are all risks you need to be aware of. One bite from a venomous animal could lead to serious illness and injury, and some can even lead to death within a matter of hours. Poisonous frogs with toxins in their skin can lead to delirium, among other forms of sickness, both neurological and physical. Even something as simple as a mosquito infected with an illness can be fatal if it bites you, and you become infected with that illness. You must be aware of the fact that predators are not always large, obvious mammals that have big teeth and menacing claws. In fact, many predators don't look like that at all. You must be aware of what is around you and always focus on keeping distance between yourself and other living beings. Even if something seems harmless, stay away. You never know what it is carrying, or how it may affect you.

The most obvious way to protect yourself from predators is to stay away from them. However, that may not always be enough. Keeping a large knife on hand and within reach is always a good idea, as it gives you direct access to a weapon that you can use should you need to fight off an animal physically. Throwing rocks and sticks at an animal, yelling at them, and staying near fire is a great way to protect yourself. If you lack tools for protection, you need to make yourself seem bigger and scarier than the animal that is taunting you, as this prevents them from trying to attack you. If you do have tools like bear mace, use them. However, you should beware that this may not always work on all species of animals.

Another way to keep yourself safe is to keep your shoes tightly tied, tuck in your clothes so insects cannot get into them, and keep your sleeping bag wrapped tightly around you to avoid making an entrance for insects. As well, before ever getting into your shelter, sleeping bag, or any other sit down or lie down location, or enclosed space, always look for possible threats. Keep an eye out for reptiles, bugs, and small animals that may have gotten in, and safely remove them before entering yourself. This way, you are less likely to encounter an accidental bite, scratch, or other injuries that could quickly turn into a serious issue.

Keeping Yourself and Your Camp Hygienic

Hygiene is one of the most important things you can focus on in the bush. A lack of hygiene can rapidly lead to illness, either by you consuming a bacteria that makes you ill or by a seemingly minor wound becoming infected. Even scratches you cannot see with the naked eye can become infected with a staph infection, or worse, and can turn into a serious health hazard. You must keep yourself and your space hygienic at all times to avoid having any harmful bacteria introduced to your system so that your body is able to remain fit and abled for as long as it needs to be.

To keep yourself and your camp hygienic, you need to consider the likely areas where bacteria would exist and routinely sterilize them to keep them as free of bacteria as possible. This includes obvious things such as cookware and hunting tools, and less obvious things such as your clothes, your mouth, and your skin. Even your bed should be routinely sterilized to prevent bacteria from building up and causing sickness.

The first thing you need to keep hygienic is yourself. One of the most important things that many people do not realize is the importance of keeping your feet dry. You must always have a dry pair of socks and footwear on at all times. Wet feet can blister, and chronically wet feet can develop fungal infections, and those infections are nearly impossible to treat in the bush unless you have the right tools. If your infections last too long, they can turn into wounds that can become gangrenous and can cause you to die. It does not take nearly as long to reach that point as you would think, either, since you are in an area where it is challenging to maintain a truly sterile environment.

Aside from your feet, it is also important that the rest of you remain dry, too. While your feet are most at-risk, the rest of your body can develop issues if you are constantly wet, also. On wet days, stay indoors as much as possible and let yourself fully dry out before going back out to complete any chores, so your body is not constantly wet. If you can, wear layers that will prevent your skin from getting wet at all. In a dire scenario, you could make a rain poncho out of a tarp, or even out of an animal hide or a few animal hides sewn together if you need one.

Keeping your mouth sterile is important, also. Your mouth comes into contact with large amounts of bacteria, all of which are usually eliminated when you brush your teeth. If you do not have a proper toothbrush and toothpaste to clean your teeth with, you will want to drink plenty of water after each meal and swish your mouth out several times a day to keep bacteria out of your mouth. You can also look for a dogwood or sassafras tree and take some of the inner bark from that tree, then chew on it. They will become highly fibrous, and both are high in tannic acid, which is an effective antibacterial agent. You could also make a tea with dogwood or sassafras bark and use it as an antiseptic mouthwash as needed.

To keep your body clean, the best way is through smoke baths. Every time you have a campfire, be sure to intentionally stand in the smoke so your body and hair can be sterilized. Make sure you take your clothes off and do this to your naked body, as well, so your entire body is staying clean. Smoke baths are particularly useful as they will help hide your natural odor, too, which means animals are less likely to detect your scent. This means you can stay hidden longer and acts like hunting will be much easier since you will not have a distinct odor that the animals can pick up on. You can also hang your clothes and bedding in a smoky area so they take on the smoke, as this can also help keep them clean. Hang them in direct sunlight for at least two hours, too, as sunlight can kill of virtually any bacteria that may linger on them.

Keeping your hands clean in the bush is best done by finding a yucca plant, yarrow, or another plant in your area that is high in saponins. You cannot ingest saponins as they are poisonous; however, they are also known for killing off bacteria. Necessarily, saponins are soap. To use it, take a piece of the plant and get it wet and then rub it vigorously between your hands. Your hands will then be clean.

For your camp, you need to ensure that you start with the basics. Keep blood and other visible contaminants off of everything, and sterilize anything that comes into contact with blood using boiling hot water. If something, like a sewing needle, needs to come into contact with the body or a wound, ensure it is passed through fire several times or boiled first to kill off any bacteria that may be lingering. In your first aid kit you can also keep some antibacterial wipes. However, you should refrain from using those except for in dire situations as you do not want to run out of them in a low-importance situation and find yourself in need of them in something that takes higher priority.

You can also keep your camp clean by keeping everything separated. Keep hygiene products, clothing, bedding, footwear, cookware, trapping and fishing gear, safety tools, and everything else separated so that if something does become contaminated, it is more challenging for it to contaminate anything else. Wash your hands regularly when going between different things, so you are not picking up or spreading germs around. You can also routinely expose your tools and belongings to sunlight for at least two hours, as the sunlight will help kill any contaminants. Do not reuse clothes, dishes, or tools without cleaning in between as they can begin to build up with bacteria, and this can lead to illnesses being introduced to your camp.

Although you cannot perfectly clean your camp environment, do your best to keep it free of objects that may be hazardous. Remove sharp branches, sticks, and rocks, keep the ground area clean, and keep everything as organized as possible. Keep a shovel handy, and any time you have to go to the bathroom, be sure to do it at least 50-100 yards away from camp, and bury it every time. This way, you are not exposed to possible bacteria in your urine or feces, which could lead to you becoming sick and transmitting sickness to others. Doing this will also keep predators away because it will hide any scents that could attract wildlife that may be coming from your camp.

Lastly, you should have a specific first aid location that can be used for helping anyone who has fallen ill or becomes injured in any way. This location should be kept clean and organized, and absolutely nothing should take place in this location unless it is first aid related. If you can, keep a sterile tarp folded up and lay that over the first aid location before treating anything, so you are less likely to introduce or pick up any bacteria from your first aid location. It is extremely important that you are very careful about anything getting into or around your wound when you are wounded in the bush, as even a small introduction of a harmful bacteria can be fatal. Be vigilant, stay clean, and do everything you can to keep bacteria away from you and your camp members.

First Aid Skills You Need to Know

Keeping a proper first aid kit available in your camp is essential. The first aid kit should never be touched or opened unless it is actually needed. When it is opened, it should be done so carefully and by someone who has washed their hands and is in as clean of an environment as possible to prevent them from introducing bacteria to the first aid kit. There are four major first aid skills you need to have in the bush, which will allow you to navigate nearly any emergency you may face: how to treat burns, how to dress wounds, how to set broken bones, and how to deal with illness.

Treating Burns

Accidents around fires can rapidly lead to burns, and improper treatment can lead to serious wounds that can cause nasty life-threatening infections, as well as harsh scarring. Treating burns promptly and properly is essential when it comes to keeping yourself or the affected individual safe.

The first thing to do is to stop the burning process. Even if the heat has been removed from the area, the skin itself will still be burning, so you need to stop this process. If you have cool filtered water, carefully run it over the burn. If not, you need to cover the burn and submerge the arm into cool water without having the water get into the burn itself to avoid contamination with bacteria or parasites.

If you can, elevate the burn to reduce swelling that could be sustained from the burn injury. Then, cover the area lightly with a non-stick dressing like sterile gauze, not cotton or adhesive bandages. If you can, you need to seek medical treatment immediately. If you cannot, you need to monitor the burn. It is likely that it will remain red, blister, and turn into a wound. At that point, you can start following wound protocol to keep the burn clean and to treat the resulting wound. If the burn reaches this point, it is likely that scarring will occur.

Dressing Wounds

Dressing wounds is important, as you need to know how to properly clean the area, treat it, and keep it covered to prevent harmful bacteria from being introduced. If you have a deeper wound, you want to let it bleed for a few minutes as the blood rushing out of the wound will push any bacteria out, too. However, you do not want to let the bleeding go on for a prolonged period of time, as this could lead to other issues related to excessive blood loss.

After a few seconds and no more than about two or three minutes, depending on the severity of bleeding (shorter bleed time for more aggressive bleeding), you need to stop the bleeding. Using gauze or your cleanest t-shirt, place it over the wound and press firmly to stop blood flow. This should allow it to begin coagulating so it can stop actively bleeding out of the wound. If you can, raise the wound above heart level, as this will make it easier for it to stop bleeding. Pressure should be applied for at least 10 minutes to stop the bleeding. If it isn't stopping the bleeding, you may need to insert your fingers, locate the severed vein or artery, and apply pressure this way to stop the bleeding.

Next, you need to clean the wound. Do this by removing the dressing for a few moments and flushing the wound with filtered drinking water from 1-2 inches away, at an angle perpendicular to the wound. You should use at least 8 ounces of water, though you may need more if the wound is covered in dirt and debris from the injury itself.

Now you need to assess the wound and decide how to cover it. Scrapes will not be able to be pulled back together, so covering them with a sterile bandage is the best option. Ripped skin, animal bites, or punctures can often be pulled back together using duct tape, stitch-style bandages, or sutures. You may also be able to superglue them together if you have access to this in your kit but only do this if it is a clean cut; otherwise, it could cause you to seal bacteria inside the wound. If an injury looks more like a chunk has been removed, you will need to moisten gauze with potable water and pack the wound with it before dressing it so that nothing can get into the wound.

Lastly, you need to dress the wound. To do this, moisten a pad with antibiotic ointment and place it over the wound. Then, cover it with a dry pad, and finally use self-adhesive tape or something similar to keep the pads in place. Now, you need to get medical help as soon as possible, if possible, because life-threatening infections can set in, in as little as six hours.

Setting Broken Bones

Broken bones in the woods can be highly dangerous. They make it so you are unable to reasonably navigate the woods, and they can leave you at risk of malformation if the bone does not heal properly, or illness if the wound becomes infected during the healing process. If a broken bone has occurred in the head, neck, or back, the only course of action is to stabilize the person and get help immediately, do not try to move the person because it could result in further damage.

If the bone is sticking out of the skin, if the bleeding will not stop or is spurting like a fountain, or if there is a loss of feeling or warmth at or beyond the injured area, prompt medical attention is also required. There is no safe way to treat this level of trauma in the bush, as the affected individual can die from either shock, improperly set bones, or infection getting deep into the body through the wound.

The first thing you must do with any broken bone is stop the bleeding, if there is bleeding occurring. If there is any bone sticking out or pushing through the skin, do not try to touch it or push it back in place as you could cause serious damage in the process. After the bleeding has stopped, you need to splint the area if possible. At this point, you want to remove any clothing from the area and apply the splint directly to the affected limb, though you do not want to move the broken bone, so if you have to, you need to cut the clothes away from the break. Then, you need to gently tape the fractured bone to a rolled-up piece of paper, a stick, or a rolled-up piece of clothing that will help keep the bone more stable. The joint above and below should be included in the splint if possible. Never try to force or twist the limb back into place, and never try to move it unless it is absolutely necessary because doing so could cause further injury.

Next, you need to do what you can to reduce swelling and prevent further injury to the place by applying an ice pack and elevating the injury if possible. If you have any, you can administer ibuprofen, acetaminophen, or naproxen. Do not give aspirin to anyone under 18 years old. As soon as you can, get medical attention, as broken bones are not easily managed in the wilderness.

Dealing With Illness

Illness can strike for many reasons, and during a survival situation, you could be at higher risk of falling ill due to the fact that you are stressed, and your body is struggling to cope with the stress. When you fall ill in the bush, you need to treat your symptoms as soon as possible, as illness can rapidly become dangerous. For example, if you have diarrhea or are vomiting, you could become seriously dehydrated in as little as twelve to twenty-four hours. If you have a stomach ache, your inability to eat could lead to additional symptoms caused by your lack of incoming nutrients when your body needs them most. Even a headache can be difficult, as headaches can make getting daily tasks done far more challenging and can leave you unable to acquire the resources you need. Further, when you are ill, it is far more challenging to mask your scent and protect yourself from predators, which leaves you especially vulnerable.

In the wilderness, treating these conditions requires you to sip potable water as often as possible. You can also take some charcoal from the bottom of the fire and drink it in a glass of water, though you do not want to drink too much as this would not be good. A small teaspoon in a glass of water can help flush any toxins out of your digestive system, though it may cause you to experience more diarrhea and vomiting for a short period of time as the toxins are being flushed out. Sipping tea made of sassafras, yarrow, brambles, nettles, plantain, ground ivy, cleavers, clover, or mallow can also help settle an upset stomach to prevent further diarrhea or vomiting.

If you have a headache, sipping tea made from willow bark can be helpful, as willow bark is said to be nature's aspirin. It contains analgesic properties that help reduce pain, making it easier for you to get over a painful headache or even dull aches in your body from days of hard work.

Foraging for Medicinal Plants

Foraging for plants that have medicinal value is similar to foraging for plants that you can consume. The safest way to do so is to have a foraging book designed for your unique geographical location, and that contains valuable information that shows you what to forage, and how, and that shows you how to avoid foraging for the wrong thing. As well, foraging with a local herbalist or wildcrafter is a great idea as they are trained in the local flora. These professionals can show you what the medicinal plants are in your location, where to find them, and how to use them.

CHAPTER 10

The Great Escape

Knowing how to escape when escape is needed is as important as knowing how to survive once you have already escaped. One wrong step during your escape could lead to you and your family being exposed to even greater dangers, or possibly dying due to the impending threat, because you took a wrong step. Often, emergencies require careful consideration and approaches, two things that are extremely hard to navigate when you are already highly stressed out. As soon as you become stressed out, your body naturally slips into fight or flight response, or worse, freeze or faint. At this point, convincing yourself to do anything may seem challenging, including escaping an emergency situation. The best way to prepare yourself for any escape, whether you need to escape indoors or escape to the wilderness, is to rehearse what needs to happen and engage in repetition by reminding yourself of the process over and over again. This way, when the emergency strikes, hopefully, your instinct kicks in, and you follow those repeated patterns and get yourself, and your family, safely removed from the emergency.

Escaping Minor Emergencies

Escaping minor emergencies requires you to escape the immediate vicinity of danger. Most minor emergencies will not require more than maybe 100 feet to 100 yards of space between yourself and the emergency to keep yourself safe. For example, if you are inside your house and a fire breaks out, you need to escape to the outdoors. Alternatively, if you are outside of your house and a thunderstorm strikes or a heavy windstorm kicks up, you need to get indoors.

Escaping a minor emergency truly depends on what emergency you are escaping, and what sort of threat that emergency poses. If you need to escape your house, you should have several clear escape routes planned so that you can run away from the danger, while safely bringing your family with you. This way, if something were to happen like a fire or a dangerous flood, you could quickly remove yourself from your house.

If you need to escape into your house, you should have a plan for where you will go. For example, in the event of a serious storm, you want to get indoors and stay away from possible hazards. Often, this means staying away from windows, doors, and open fireplaces with chimneys. If you are facing a serious windstorm or a tornado, you want to get to the lowest floor in your house and hide as far away from any heavy furniture as possible, as well as away from windows, doors, and fireplaces with chimneys. Your furnace, electrical wires, and gas lines also need to be inspected as even seemingly small or non-observed disasters can damage these, and they can be life-threatening.

Escaping Major Emergencies

If you are in a major emergency and you need to escape your city, you must be ready to escape safely. Prepare for your escape with a full tank of gas in your vehicle or with arrangements to meet up with someone who has a vehicle and can help you escape if you do not drive. You should also have your G'n'G bags packed and ready to go. Your larger bags may be at home, but you should have smaller bags with you in your car at all times so that if you have to escape and cannot return home first, you can escape with what you have and still have at least a few things to help you get started.

As soon as you have everything and are on the road, you need to take the most direct route out of the city as you possibly can. The route may be thick with people also trying to escape, so be patient and move as quickly as you can without risking yourself or anyone else, as car accidents are not ideal at this point in time. For some emergencies, it can be particularly scary. For example, in some cases, people are driving away from their hometowns while wildfires are on the side of the road they are driving on, or are driving away just hours before a major hurricane is due to hit. Either way, you need to be as patient as possible.

It is important to understand that when you are escaping from your city, there is a time to leave, and then there is a time to stay. You need to leave early enough that you actually have time to escape, even with all of the gridlock that may be happening on local roads. Otherwise, you might find yourself in even more danger as you are trapped in your car when disaster strikes. It is vital that you listen to emergency warnings and that you heed those warnings as soon as possible. With any luck, you escape well enough in advance that you are safe, and you can stay with friends or family elsewhere who are not set to be affected by the disaster. If the disaster is a pandemic or the enforcement of a police state, it may make more sense to skip trying to stay with anyone and instead head to the wilderness to set up camp and keep to yourself until everything becomes safer.

If you must stay, or if you escape, but without enough time, you will likely find yourself facing a disaster where you have to embrace your wilderness skills to protect yourself and your family. In this case, the first step for escaping is to keep yourself safe while the disaster strikes. Find somewhere safe to be, such as a storm cellar, or somewhere that is covered with a steady, strong building that is unlikely to collapse. Avoid hiding around vehicles, under trees, near furniture that could fall down, near windows or doors, or on the level of a house that has the roof in case the roof is damaged in the storm. If heavy flooding is present, without wind storms or lightning, you may need to get to higher ground either by heading to the highest floor in your house or even getting up onto your roof to stay away from the flooding. Weather the storm using your G'n'G bag and listening to updates that will inform you as to what is going on and what you can do to keep yourself safe. Always pay close attention to radio updates, as authorities will let you know what you can do to stay safe and will use the radio to broadcast where you can go or how you can get relief if you are trapped or in need of rescuing.

Once the disaster is done, you need to assess the damage and decide your course of action. If you are able to safely stay in your home location, you can stay there. Otherwise, you may need to commence your escape once the storm has passed so that you can either go stay elsewhere or stay in the wilderness in a safer location until it is safer for you to return home.

CHAPTER 11

The Unspoken Essential Of Survival

One unspoken essential of survival that almost no one talks about also happens to be one of the most influential aspects of your survival. In fact, if you do not manage this particular aspect of your survival, you can completely lose the ability to survive and may find yourself floundering or even dying in a situation where it may have been perfectly feasible to survive. If you watch any of the reality shows on TV that focus on survival skills, you likely already know what this unspoken essential of survival is, as many of the contestants on those shows come across it and find themselves quitting prematurely. That is, your mindset.

If you are in the wilderness, your mindset must be focused on survival, as a mindset focused on anything else can lead to distractions and increased challenges placed on your survival. Focusing on everything going wrong, rather than everything you can do to protect yourself, elevates your stress, and makes necessary survival techniques far more challenging. Some people in real survival situations will even die because of the stress itself. In many cases of rescue missions where entire groups were stranded, there have been instances where one or two people passed away either due to suicide or due to a lack of will to survive, which ultimately cost them their lives. You *must* learn how to strengthen your will and reinforce your mindset if you are going to survive dangerous situations. Without your mindset on board, predators and nasty bacteria are minor dangers in comparison to what you are up against.

The Biggest Danger Lurking At Two AM

In the wilderness, there is a time of day that is known as being the darkest hour. That is, at two AM. All day long, survivalists are focused on fulfilling tasks essential to their survival and are playing an active role in their wellbeing, and the wellbeing of those they are stranded with. This active role results in them feeling as though they have some sense of control over their situation, and like all will be okay because they are able to keep themselves going. Unfortunately, at two AM, there is no active role. You are supposed to be sleeping. You may have even been sleeping until something woke you up.

Once you are awake, it is easy for the reality of what you are going through to set in, and with nothing to keep you active or busy, it can be challenging to move those thoughts out of your mind. On reality TV, countless conversations about these hardships and giving up have been recorded and shared for thousands to see. What people don't realize is that off of reality TV, in real survival settings, thousands more of these conversations have actually happened, and many have ended in people not surviving to see the next day, or not surviving through to see the rescue mission.

At 2 AM, when everything else is calm, you must focus on one thing, and one thing only: getting back to sleep. Your body needs your rest, and you need the break from everything you are up against. Allowing yourself to stay awake, pondering the many things you are facing will only lead to you feeling a greater sense of stress and burden, which will ultimately drive you into the depths of depression and anxiety. For some people, hysteria sets in, and that in and of itself can be a highly dangerous place to be in.

It may seem like an impossible discipline to reel your mind back into a state of control, but it is essential if you are going to survive. You need to learn how to shut down thoughts, refuse to entertain your fears, and focus exclusively on the survival mission at hand. Until you are rescued, your only job is to get from one day to the next, one hour to the next, or one minute to the next, whatever you can handle.

Most people never come across such intense survival experiences in their lives. As a result, they are totally unprepared for the serious mental strength it takes, and for the dangers that can be lurking in their thoughts. If you have never had to withstand this, then you can consider yourself lucky. However, one day you might have to endure it, and if you do, you need to be ready for that 2 AM dread. Being aware of it in advance can help you realize that what you are thinking and feeling is normal, and can help you switch into refusing the thoughts and going back to sleep because you know that this is the healthiest choice you can make. Even if you don't know when you will be rescued, or if you have lost so much, your job is not to focus on that now. Your job is to focus on survival, and the rest can come later. 2 AM is never the right time to sort through your thoughts or your problems. Go to sleep.

Keeping Yourself on Track for Survival

People who survive the wilderness share one thing in common: survival mode. They fiercely click into survival mode and do not stop to question themselves or their actions, because they know they must take them. This lessens their emotional stress and increases their ability to take necessary action for survival. They are worried solely about surviving every single day, period. As a result, their body is able to kick into survival mode with them, and they end up surviving virtually anything they come up against, short of a freak accident or a tragic illness or injury in the bush, which leads to their death.

If you are in the bush, you have to remember that as a human, you are a part of the animal kingdom. Just like every other animal in that bush, you have access to a powerful instinct inside of you that will tell you what to do, where to look, how to move, where to go, and how to keep yourself and anyone else with you alive. Even if you have no idea what you are doing, if you lean into that instinct, it will help you out a lot more than you may expect. Even though we live our modern lives extremely different from the animals in the bush, we are still animals, and we are not nearly as far removed from our instincts as people tend to believe we are.

As soon as you allow yourself to lean into that survival, you will notice that all of your priorities change. Rather than worrying about the past or the future, as humans often do, you will be solely worried about the present. Your instincts will sharpen as your awareness heightens, your ability to navigate difficult terrain is increased, and your understanding of how to survive in the bush seems to come naturally. You will easily spot threats that come your way, you will seemingly "know" how to handle difficult situations, and you will know how to shut out the challenging emotions and keep yourself focused.

In survival mode, none of the emotions matter anymore; only your survival does. You can worry about snapping out of it and healing from all of this later on when the chance arrives. For now, just focus on surviving.

CHAPTER 12

Getting Help When Needed

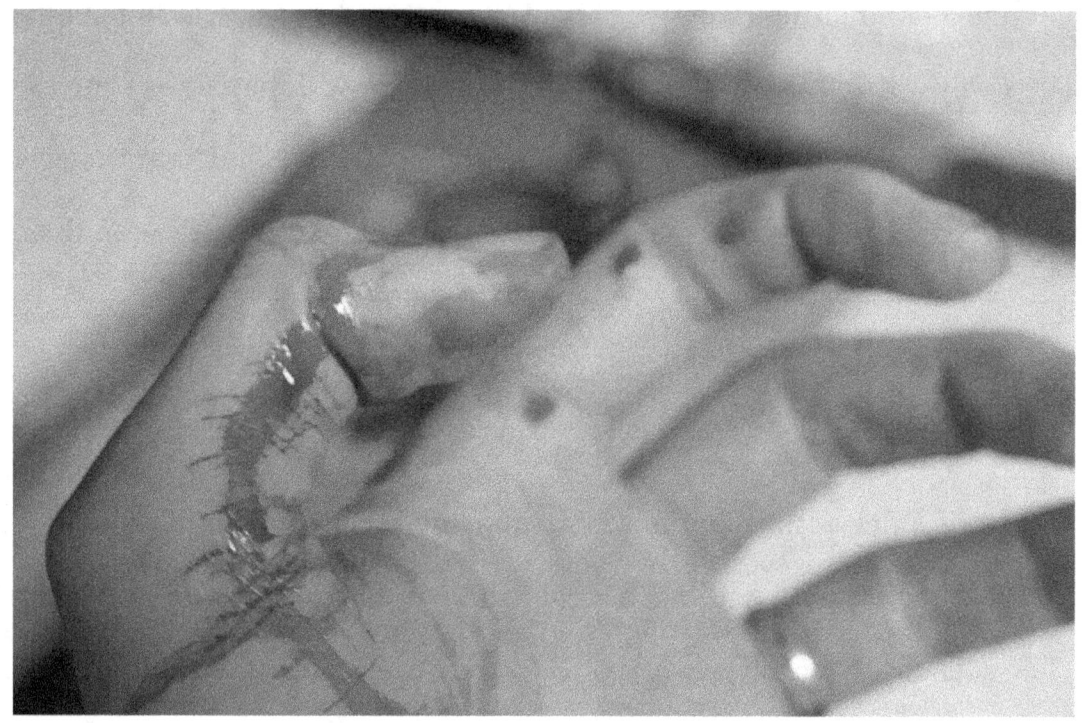

When you are in a survival setting, there are times when you will need to call for help, and times when you won't. Knowing how to determine when is the right time to call, and who to call, is important as it will ensure that you get access to the safety you need as soon as possible. It is also important to understand what needs to be done after calling for help to ensure that anyone who might be coming to help you knows where to find you, what they need to help you, and how to get the job done. The more you can prepare your rescuers for what they are coming to, the easier it will be for them to rescue you safely.

When Is the Right Time to Call?

Knowing when to call for help is important. Amid an emergency situation, it may be hard to determine when you should make that call, or if a call even needs to be made in the first place. For some people, the minute they begin to feel panic, they begin to dial for help, even though that may not be necessary. For others, they might try to engage in a rescue mission alone without calling for help because they don't think there is time, or the emergency itself causes them to completely forget that help is available. Both calling for help when none is needed, or forgetting or refusing to call for help when it is needed, are bad situations to be in.

When you find yourself in an emergency, it is important to pause and ask yourself a few questions about what is going on right now. Is it reasonable for you to navigate this emergency on your own? Or is this something that would be better left to professionals? This may be obvious if you are in a situation where someone has scraped their knee, or where your house is on fire. With a scraped knee, you can easily manage that yourself with your first aid kit, whereas when your house is on fire, it is obvious that you need to call 911. But what if your emergency is something like a serious cut that is bleeding or a severed digit? When it comes to serious emergencies, you must ask yourself how reasonable it is for you to handle this emergency on your own, versus calling for help.

If the injured or affected individual is stable, despite their injury, you may be able to drive them to the hospital yourself. If you can, do this, as it will relieve pressure on emergency services and will also help you save the money it costs to hire emergency transportation services. Further, driving directly to the hospital yourself is faster than having someone drive all the way to your house then to the hospital, even if they are speeding. If the person is not stable or cannot be stabilized, call for help. This means if someone is drowning, if someone has been knocked unconscious and is not waking up, if they are too weak to move, or if it would be dangerous or extremely challenging for you to move them, you call for help.

In some cases, you may be able to rely on the help of a doctor's appointment, or on a simple call to your doctor's office to ensure that you have handled things properly. For example, if you get food poisoning and are quite sick, but are not dehydrated, you can call your doctor or book an appointment without having to call an emergency line. These types of emergencies do need to be handled the right way, but they are not so pressing that you have to call for immediate help.

Always be sure to call the right level of help for your situation, because calling the wrong level of help could lead to you tying up precious resources, having unnecessary expenses to pay, and possibly wasting people's time. Alternatively, not calling the right level of help for your situation could lead to the person who has been affected to fail to receive the necessary level of care that they require. As a result, they could become further injured or ill because the rescue team was ill prepared to deal with the specific situation you are facing.

Who Is the Right Person to Call?

Knowing the right person to call is important. When you are in an emergency, it can be challenging to know who to call as you will be experiencing a great deal of stress and that stress can make navigating your situation seemingly impossible. For this reason, it can be helpful to have a list of specific emergency contacts and numbers you can call in any range of emergencies, as this list will help you know exactly who to call for any given situation. You should keep this list in your G'n'G bag, and another in your car. Keep it laminated or otherwise protected so that if you need it, you are not at risk of grabbing the paper only to find out it has been torn, smudged, or otherwise damaged.

The emergency numbers you should have on hand include any in case of emergency contacts that are relevant to your family, such as your spouse, parents, siblings, or other family members.

You should also have the numbers for:

- Local fire department
- Local police department (non-emergency line)
- C
- oast guard
- Family doctor
- Nurse line
- Nearby hospitals

- Local EMS
- Poison control
- Veterinarian
- Water company
- Power company
- Tow truck
- Animal control
- Locksmith
- Next door neighbors
- Insurance agent
- Important co-workers
- Boss
- Important family members

These numbers are all people you might have to call in an emergency, and having their numbers readily written down means you do not have to go looking for them when the time comes. This can also help you discover the right person to call right away, as you can gauge the level of emergency and call the appropriate number. For example, if you or your family member is experiencing symptoms of possible illness, you could call your family doctor to book an appointment. If they are showing symptoms of illness that cannot wait for an appointment, you can call your local nurse line. If they are showing even bigger symptoms, you can call the hospital and bring them in to be checked. Or, if they are showing symptoms that are so bad that you cannot get them to the hospital yourself, you can call for EMS. Always gauge your call appropriately and call the right people, so you have the right help for the job, as this is key to navigating any emergency quickly and with success. Calling the wrong people could result in you not having the right help that is needed, and that could lead to the emergency growing or becoming more serious as time passes. In emergencies, time is of the essence, so be quick, be accurate, and call for help when you need it.

How Can You Prepare to Be Rescued?

Calling for help may require some preparation on your end when it comes to readying yourself to be rescued. There are different preparation methods required depending on what you are doing, so you want to make sure you have everything you need for your rescue mission on hand.

If you are at home and need rescuing, make sure you are in a place where your rescuers can easily locate you. Be clear about where you are, what help is needed, and how they can find you. In the instance of a house fire or damage to the inside of your home, get outside and wait on the lawn or sidewalk for the rescue team to arrive, so they do not have to rescue you from indoors. If you cannot escape, tell your rescue team where you are so they can quickly access you and remove you from the dangerous location. If you are dealing with something like a serious injury or illness, make sure doors are unlocked, and rescuers know to come in if they can, move the affected individual to the front door if possible, or have someone ready to answer the door when they arrive.

In an outdoor emergency, such as if you are surviving in the wilderness, you may need to find your way to a clearing, to a major road, or to some other form of landmark that is easily accessible by rescuers so you can be rescued. While rescue teams can retrieve you from virtually anywhere because of the high tech gear they carry, it is easier for them to rescue you if you are in an area where they can quickly gain access to. As you wait for your rescue team to come find you, try to get to a clearing or a large landmark, and let your rescue team know that this is your plan. Let them know where you are leaving from, too, so they know where they can find you if you do not make it to the clearing. Never go anywhere that your rescuers do not know you are going, and always tell them where you have been, where you are coming from, and where you are heading. This way, you are able to be saved quicker. If you use a device that GPS pings your location to your rescue team, *do not leave that location.* Even if it is not optimal for being rescued, it is where the rescue team knows to find you, and if you leave that location, they will not be able to find you. *Stay there.*

Is There Ever a Time When You Should Not Call?

There are certain times when you should *not* call for help, even if you are in need of some form of help. The most important one to consider is relevant when you are in a large-scale emergency, but you may not be in a pressing emergency yourself. For example, let's say your town gets hit by a hurricane, and your neighborhood was affected. Perhaps your house has been damaged, or someone in your family has sustained a minor injury, but it is something you can deal with from home. In this case, you should not be in a rush to call for help as doing so can tie up resources for people who were also struck by the hurricane and who might be trapped in dire situations. Those other people may be seriously injured, they may be trapped, or they may otherwise be in serious danger. If you can keep yourself safe for a while, try to sustain yourself for as long as you can until you truly need help, then call for it. Use a sign in your window that either says "Here, Need Immediate Help" or "Here, No Help Needed," depending on your situation. In either case, rescue crews will know where you are and will be able to prioritize your rescue accordingly based on your level of need. This way, more serious situations are helped first, and those who can sustain themselves for a while longer do not put strain on the rescue crews.

Another time when you might not call for help is when you are in a situation where help cannot do anything, or where help may actually be more dangerous than anything else. For example, many countries have found themselves falling into police states, and they cannot rely on help because that help may actually do more harm than good. In this case, you must seriously assess the emergency and do everything you can to navigate it yourself. If you really cannot, take the person who has endured the emergency and a burner phone, move that person far away from where you are staying, call for help on the burner phone, and leave it with that person. This way, they get the help they need, and you are not at risk of being found and hurt by the police state. While this may seem harsh or you may fear losing that person, it is ultimately better than them suffering without a lack of access to adequate resources and help for their condition.

CONCLUSION

Being in a survival situation can be scary, especially if you do not know what you are getting into. Many people do not realize that you could find yourself inside a serious survival mission within an urban environment, possibly even within your home. Others may be more "traditional" in the sense that you need to escape your home and live in the wilderness for a while until it is safe for you to return.

Knowing how to survive in any situation is important, as it is the first step in getting help and finding your way back to safety. If you fail to survive, you will fail to get the help you need as there will be no more helping you. Many people think the emergency itself is the leading cause of death, but the inability to survive the aftermath also carries a huge death toll. For example, if you find yourself launched into the wilderness after a natural disaster strikes, not knowing how to catch and prepare food or purify water for consumption could lead to your death. These dangers are just as bad as the emergency itself, so you must discover how to properly navigate them and keep yourself safe until you can return to a safer environment.

I hope that through reading *Survival Guide for Beginners 2020,* you feel confident in your ability to navigate any emergency, no matter what it is. Whether you need to survive an urban environment or a wilderness environment, there are many steps you can take to keep yourself alive and safe. Knowing how to take them, and when to take them, will make all the difference.

I strongly encourage you to keep a copy of this book in your G'n'G bag so that if you ever do find yourself in an emergency, you have access to this guide, which will show you exactly how to navigate it. Sometimes, in the face of stress and fear, memory can fail us, so having a hard copy available to go back to is essential to keep you going and keep you safe even in the most dire of times.

Before you go, I also ask that you take a moment to review *Survival Guide for Beginners 2020* on Amazon Kindle. Your honest feedback would be greatly appreciated, and it will help others discover how they, too, can survive any emergency they may face in their lifetimes. This is essential knowledge, so the more people that have it, the better.

Thank you, and best of luck in any situation you may come across. Remember, stay positive, stay focused, get the job done, and keep going. You can do it.

The Beginner's Vegetable Garden 2020

Leslie Martin

© Copyright 2020 by Leslie Martin. All right reserved.

The work contained herein has been produced with the intent to provide relevant knowledge and information on the topic on the topic described in the title for entertainment purposes only. While the author has gone to every extent to furnish up to date and true information, no claims can be made as to its accuracy or validity as the author has made no claims to be an expert on this topic. Notwithstanding, the reader is asked to do their own research and consult any subject matter experts they deem necessary to ensure the quality and accuracy of the material presented herein.

This statement is legally binding as deemed by the Committee of Publishers Association and the American Bar Association for the territory of the United States. Other jurisdictions may apply their own legal statutes. Any reproduction, transmission or copying of this material contained in this work without the express written consent of the copyright holder shall be deemed as a copyright violation as per the current legislation in force on the date of publishing and subsequent time thereafter. All additional works derived from this material may be claimed by the holder of this copyright.

The data, depictions, events, descriptions and all other information forthwith are considered to be true, fair and accurate unless the work is expressly described as a work of fiction. Regardless of the nature of this work, the Publisher is exempt from any responsibility of actions taken by the reader in conjunction with this work. The Publisher acknowledges that the reader acts of their own accord and releases the author and Publisher of any responsibility for the observance of tips, advice, counsel, strategies and techniques that may be offered in this volume.

INTRODUCTION

Congratulations on purchasing *The Beginner's Vegetable Garden 2020,* and thank you for doing so.

The chapters in this book will discuss vegetable gardening and the various ways in which it can be done. If you are a beginner in gardening or just love gardening as your hobby, you should try out vegetable gardening. You will come across various skills in this book that can help you to grow vegetables on your own. The basics of gardening can be found in this book. It might be that the weather where you live is very uncertain, and it makes gardening a tough job. However, in such cases, you can still grow your own vegetables with the use of raised bed gardening, container gardening, and in-ground gardening. All these are the various ways in which you can grow vegetables on your own despite the climate or other factors that might not be in your favor.

Each type of gardening comes with its own set of pros and cons, and I am going to walk you through all of it in this book. With the growing uncertainty of this world along with a rise in world population, growing your own vegetables is turning out to be an essential job. Everything that you need to know for setting up your garden has been included in this book.

There are plenty of books on this subject on the market, thanks again for choosing this one! Every effort was made to ensure it is full of as much useful information as possible, and please enjoy!

CHAPTER 1

Raised Bed Gardening

Some people might think that you need a large yard in order to be able to grow a useful garden. This simply just isn't the case. There are many places all around you that would suffice for you to grow your own garden. Take a look along the edge of the alley or beside the driveway. You can grow vegetables and food everywhere if you can adapt the space properly.

One such adaptation is raised bed gardening. Even when you do not have much time for setting up your garden, you can still have the chance to develop a productive garden of veggies. Not sure how to do that? Don't worry; I am going to explain it all to you. Raised bed gardening can be regarded as the best shortcut for a plentiful harvest. It involves developing raised spaces where you can grow your own plants. You can build your garden anywhere with the help of raised beds. Moreover, you can grow more food in a very confined space. The plants can be placed very close to one another, and each square inch can be made productive.

You can either build your own raised bed or just get one from the market. This will be discussed in the upcoming chapters. But how many raised beds you are required to have for starting? In case you have limited space or time, you can start with one. If you want to increase the vegetable yield with time, you will need more beds. If you are new to the world of gardening, start small. It is always better to get thrilled with all that you can grow in a small-sized garden. Otherwise, it can make you frustrated by the commitment of time that is required by the big ones. Also, it makes more sense to learn the basics of gardening first before you invest your money and time in your hobby. As you start with this, you will soon be getting an idea as to the time that this new endeavor is going to use up from your daily schedule. You will come to know whether you like to spend time watering, planting, and weeding.

A great size for setting up your beginner's garden is 8 x 8 feet. Try keeping it as simple as possible. For starters, do not select more than 3 – 4 types of vegetables. As you start simple, you will be able to get a great amount of produce for summer meals. It will be easier for you to keep up with the gardening chores as well. If you are feeling confused regarding which vegetables to start with, you can start with the ones that you love the most. It can be tomatoes, onions, potatoes, etc. Before you commence, think about the quantity of produce that you want. Try to be realistic about the number of plants or seeds that you will need to reach your target. You can opt for vegetables that can be harvested several times, such as peppers and squash.

If possible, try to opt for both warm and cool weather vegetables. By doing this, you can get a harvest of fresh vegetables continuously through all the seasons. When it is early spring, you can opt for lettuce, peas, broccoli, and carrots. For the hot season, you can plant eggplants, tomatoes, herbs, and peppers. For the cool season, you can plant cabbage, kale, and potatoes. Also, while choosing the spot, try to be thoughtful about the requirements of the garden. Make sure that everything is handy from the spot of your garden. Try to create a checklist that will contain the essentials such as water, sun, drainage, storage, etc. You will also have to ensure that the spot is not prone to insects and pests. The plants will have to be protected from strong winds, heavy rain, and other natural features.

Let us start with the basics of raised bed gardening first, and then we will slowly progress to the other components of the same.

Basics

Just like other types of gardening, raised bed gardening also needs some of the essentials such as sunlight, water, drainage, logistics, etc. You will need to ensure that your garden is getting all that it needs to provide you with the best results.

Sun

Like all other types of plants, vegetables also need enough sunlight to start the process of photosynthesis. Photosynthesis helps in transforming the energy of sunlight into glucose that is used by the plants for making other substances like cellulose and starch. Starch is used as the source of food, while cellulose is needed for building the cellular walls. Vegetables that come with fast-growing speed will need sunlight for about 6 – 8 hours every day. The sunlight needs to be direct without any form of blockage from fences, trees, or shrubs. That is the reason why you might not succeed in your venture of gardening if you plant vegetables that are sun-loving in shady spots.

In case the spot where you have decided to build your garden provides partial shade, try planting veggies and herbs that are suited for such conditions. Vegetables such as chard, kale, lettuce, cilantro, chives, thyme, and parsley do not need much sunlight. Root vegetables such as beet, radish, and carrots might also tend to work if the gardening spot can get at least 4 – 5 hours of direct light from the sun daily. For the fast-growing vegetables, try to set up your raised bed gardening at a place that can get enough sunlight all throughout the day, without shade of any kind. The fast-growing group of vegetables includes cucumber, pepper, tomato, corn, beans, peas, eggplants, etc.

Drainage

Raised bed gardening is sometimes much easier than traditional gardens. Just like the other types of gardening, raised bed gardening also needs proper drainage. It is needed for promoting optimal growth of plants and also for preventing rotting of roots. Having an efficient system of drainage is very important. A well-organized drainage system is when the garden water can drain to the soil bottom, thus preventing water clogging near the root area of the plants. When there is an absence of proper drainage, the plants might not be able to grow properly. Rotting of the roots might occur when excessive water stores up near the root area because of the lack of a proper system of drainage. Without adequate drainage, a plant will tend to die slowly. The best way of preventing this is by having a well-planned system of drainage.

Raised bed garden does not come with a bottom and sits on the ground directly. If you have set up a raised bed garden that is taller or knee-height, you will have some extra number of steps for ensuring proper drainage of the garden. Raised bed garden, which is lower than knee-height, will have drainage from the dirt area beneath the garden bed. So, for avoiding standing water in the garden, you will need to place soil for planting the vegetables on the dirt to ensure perfect drainage. You will also need to use certain materials at the bed bottom for making the setup perfect. Pea rocks, stones, and crushed granite can be used. There is something that you have to make sure while placing any of these materials - it is at least 3 inches in depth or more for raising the bed higher. After you have placed the base rocks, you can place soil on top of it. The rocks as the base will ensure drainage of water while preventing planting soil from becoming compact with time.

Water

Smart watering is the secret to the success of gardening. It works specifically in all those places where the weather is dry and warm. In the first week after germination of the seeds or after transplantation of the seedlings, you will need to water the plants frequently for making them strong. After the plants have grown properly, you will need to provide them with a long drink after every few days in place of small showers every day. The water will be moving in deeper into the plant soil, and that will result in deeper growth of the roots. With deeper roots, the plants will be able to take in the required amount of nutrients and will be able to stay healthy.

Your watering schedule will depend on several factors, such as the composition of the soil and your climate. Clay soil will tend to dry out much faster when compared to sandy soil. Windy and sunny weather tends to dry out soil faster than cloudy and cool weather. Not sure about watering requirements? Try to feel the soil about 4 – 5 inches down from the surface of the garden. If the soil feels dry, it is time for watering. This needs to be done during the rainy season as well. This is because sometimes rainwater might just run off the growing surface rather than getting soaked in the soil. You can add compost to the soil for improving its ability to supply the plants with the required amount of water.

Adding compost to your garden is like adding up sponges to a surface. Water will run through, but some amount of water will also get soaked in the layer of compost. Also, with the help of compost, you will be able to make soil aerated. Thus it will be able to provide better drainage. Plants take in oxygen with the help of roots and are most likely to drown if the soil remains soggy for many days. During hot weather, plants might tend to wilt because of the heat. But, it is not the indication of being deprived of moisture. As you check the soil, you will get to know the actual story.

If you think that your garden needs more water, there are various options for doing so. You can use a watering wand to deliver more water at a faster rate. In case you are away from the garden for a long period, you can get a water timer. It will help in turning on the soaker hose or sprinkler. In order to keep the growing plants productive and healthy, do not allow the soil to get dried out completely. Also, plants that are water-stressed might tend to get tough and bitter in taste. So, make sure that you determine the schedule of watering properly. Try to prevent yourself from overwatering the plants.

Tip: Try to build the garden near the water source. It will help in easing your task.

Logistics

You will need to look after the logistics to ensure easy and frequent access to the garden. Make sure that you have enough feasibility and space for using a garden cart or wheelbarrow, logistics for putting away and bringing tools along with materials, distance for moving amendments from your vehicle to shade, proximity of irrigation or hand-watering, and patterns of foot traffic to ensure harvesting and maintenance. It is very important to keep paths around the garden. It might reduce the space of the garden. But, without having enough space in the surrounding might make the whole task of gardening a bit tough. Plan the beds of gardening that can fit the size of your body to ensure comfort. Ensure that you can reach one side form the other with ease. You can also test run the garden to be sure that it is functional and also comfortable for you.

While planning out your garden, consider the future problems of pests. It is especially important in those areas where there is a pest population nearby, such as gophers, rats, rabbits, squirrels, etc. Will the location that you have chosen permit you to install fencing or enclosures of wire around the garden to protect the plants from pets or wildlife? Try to avoid slopes. Gardening in a sloped area, especially raised bed gardening, might result in draining out of the soil very quickly. Also, it will make the task of watering and planting tougher. There is no reason for getting hard on your back and muscles. When you decide to opt for organic gardening, it will produce a considerable amount of waste material. So, it would be better for you if you set up the garden bed away from the entrance of your home, sidewalks, pool, and seating area.

Gardening in the front yard is accepted and even encouraged by the authorities in various areas. So, try to consider the growing factors first before opting for a place of gardening. Make sure that you check the regulations of the local authorities to avoid problems of any kind in the near future.

Size

The primary goal of having a raised bed garden is to ease the need of the gardeners to step into the garden. In simple words, the garden needs to be easily accessible from all sides. The perfect size of a raised bed garden will be 4 feet wide for the adults and 3 feet wide for children. The length of the garden bed is not as critical, as much as the width of the bed is. But, keep in mind that excessively long garden beds might turn out to be a hassle for walking around. You might also feel a bit tough to work on a large garden. It is true that the length of a raised bed garden will be determined partly by the materials that are available. But, keep a note that the overall lumber cost will increase if you build the garden bed more than 10 – 12 feet in length.

The higher you can build the garden bed, the more soil you will need. This will ultimately be adding to the labor and cost that are involved in the project. If you plan to build a high garden bed, make sure that it is strong enough from the base to tackle the weight of the soil. There are certain considerations that you will need to keep in mind.

- There are certain vegetables that required at least 8 – 10 inches of soil for thriving. In case the height of the bed is lower than the mentioned size, dig the remaining soil below the surface of the bed.
- In case the raised bed is placed on a hard surface, the minimum height mark of 8 – 10 inches might not be deep enough for certain crops, for example, potatoes.
- To permit wheelchair access, you will need to make the bed at least 24 inches tall.
- You can consider setting up gardening beds of various heights for accommodating gardeners of different sizes.

You should take care of the garden orientation as well. But, it won't be much of a problem if enough space is provided between the gardening beds for access. The tall crop will tend to shade the shorter crops that are behind them if crops of all sizes are planted on the same bed.

You will have to plan from the beginning if you want to get new lumber. Lumber generally comes in sizes of 8-, 10-, and 12-feet lengths. So, you can keep the dimension of the garden beds to multiples of 3 or 2 feet for minimizing the waste. For instance, if you are willing to set up a bed of 3 feet by 6 feet, lumber of 12 feet will be perfect.

If you are starting new, you can proceed with small-sized gardening beds. The thickness of the walls will rely on the type of material you use. It is needed to be completely aware of the individual dimensions of each of the garden beds along with the complete plan layout. For example, concrete blocks that are 8 inches in thickness will be taking up more space and will also need more distance for reaching across. Wooden planks that are thick by one-inch will need vertical support after every 3 – 4 feet. Make sure that the surface on which you set up the bed is completely flat. So, you will need to level the frame at the time of installing. For avoiding an excessive amount of excavation, if the place is sloped, you can install garden beds of the shortest dimension that is perpendicular to the slope, such as stair steps. Also, you can alter the shape of the bed according to your space and need.

Building Structures

Building elevated growing areas for growing vegetables is easier than it actually looks. You are required to decide a couple of things, such as the kind of wood you want to use, the height of the bed, whether you want to use pre-made braces for the corners, and so on. As you divide every segment of your raised bed garden, it will help in simplifying the overall construction process. You can opt for concrete blocks or some other material for the growing bed. But, lumber is always available and is cost-effective too.

In the majority of the cases, cedar is preferred as the perfect wood for building a raised bed. This is because cedar is resistant to rot. You can also opt for redwood in the place of cedar. However, redwood is not as abundant as cedar.

As you start with building your raised bed garden, you will need to first determine the spot. In case you have decided to place the bed in the yard, remove grass from the area where you will be placing the bed. After you are done with removing the grass, try to loosen up the soil a bit with the help of a shovel. This is the preparation stage.

The perfect size of a raised bed for beginners is 3 feet by 6 feet and a depth of 1 foot. However, you can adjust the dimensions of the bed according to your needs. The majority of the raised beds are maximum four feet wide for allowing the gardeners to easily get to the center. The minimum depth for herbs and leafy vegetables is 6 inches and 12 inches for root vegetables. You can also eco-stain or apply oil to the woods for extending the life of the same. You can line the bed bottom with mesh net cloth to prevent burrowing animals and fit copper strips within the top edge of the bed for deterring slugs. You can also install hoops of PVC for supporting the row covers.

Materials Needed

Untreated wooden planks according to the dimensions of the garden (untreated)

3 ½ inches of #14 screws

Optional

Three by 6 feet hardware cloth for the bed bottom

18 feet copper stripping

Two PVC pipes

Tin sheet

Process

- In case you want to stain or oil the wooden boards, try to do this before setting up the system. Provide two days for allowing them to dry.

- On the surface where you want to set up the garden, set out two four by four wooden boards: Lay, one board of 3 feet, two by two on the top. Put two four by four-flush posts at the ends.
- Attach the wooden boards using the 3 ½ inch screws.
- Repeat the same process with the other wooden board. You will need to build two like this. These boards will be the short ends of the garden bed.
- Stand the sides on edge and place the 6 feet long boards of 2 by 6.
- Attach the long boards with the help of screws.
- Move the bed in place and level the surface if required.
- Attach strips of copper through the inside edge of the top of the bed for deterring slugs from getting in. You can line the base with the use of hardware cloth and attach pipes of PVC for supporting the shade clothes or row covers. (Optional)
- For making supports for the row covers, use two long pipes of PVC and attach the same to each long side of the garden bed. Secure the pipes in place with the use of screws. The pipe tubes will act as the hoop holders for the row covers.
- Fill up the bed with soil and make it ready for planting.

Various Structures

Raised beds can be designed in various structures. So, you have complete freedom of designing it the way you want. While talking about odd structures, some gardeners have started using trellis for making their raised beds. A simple nature of trellis made out of bamboo stakes and wire mesh can provide support for all your plants. The tired style of designing beds is the most famous out of all. You can design the bed in a way where the plants will be planted in different tiers or steps. You can make them rounded or flat like stairs. People are now opting for the caged version a lot for protecting the plants from animals and pests of all kinds.

Garden Covers

Also known as row cover or garden fabric, a garden cover is a great tool that can help in improving the quality of your gardening. It can be used in various ways:

- Protect the plants from strong wind and cold
- Prevents the spread of diseases and insects
- Prevent the plants and soil from getting overheated

There are various options available to you while choosing the type of row cover that you want for your garden:

- **All-purpose row cover:** They are made from polypropylene and are capable of transmitting about 75% of the available light. They can help in keeping the heat inside, prevent bugs, and can act as a superb windbreak for protecting the small plants. They can protect the plants from frost damage as well.
- **Summerweight fabric:** They are light in weight and cannot trap in much heat. They are most widely used for protecting plants from insects, birds, and diseases. They can transmit about 80% of the available light. But, they are not suitable for blocking rain or frost.

- **Garden Quilt:** They are thicker than the others and can transmit about 60% of the available light. They are used for extending the season of growing into late fall or early spring. This form of row cover is also used for insulating vegetables.

There are various other options available for row covers. You will need to determine the usage first before you opt for the final one for your raised bed garden.

Plants

If you are new to the world of gardening, it is better to start simple. When you have limited space along with time, you might have the urge to grow as many plants as you can. Every gardener grows eggplant and tomatoes in their raised beds. But, that does not mean you will start with such plants from the very beginning. Such types of plants are rewarding in nature but also need extra attention and care. Try omitting them if you are new and opt for something really simple. You can start with simple herbs like thyme and mint. They need lesser care and water as well. You can slowly level up your garden as you gain expertise in the same.

Plant Journal

No matter what type of plants you grow in your raised bed garden, try to keep a journal for the plants that you have grown. This way, you will be able to track the needs of various types of plants along with the perfect weather of growing them. While maintaining a plant journal, do not forget to mention the location of the plant where you have grown them. In this way, you will be able to track their progress as well.

You should keep a proper record of the plants that you grow in each bed. This will help you to make informed decisions about the types of amendments that the soil will need every time while planting. As each plant comes along with individual needs, you can make a table of the requirements for making your task more manageable. For example, tomatoes like to grow in soil that is rich in calcium. So, before planting other crops in a bed that has been used for growing tomatoes, it is better to treat the bed with calcium.

Understanding the Plant Needs

The primary mistake that is made by most of the beginner growers is misunderstanding the plant's needs. We all know that plants such as peppers and tomatoes need more water, more solar energy, and more nutrients from the soil. Before you start growing plants, try to do some research about the type of plants that you are going to choose. How much sunlight do the growing beds receive during the course of the day? What are the nutrient requirements of the plants? As you answer these questions to yourself before growing plants, you will be able to avoid most of the gardening failures.

Spacing

In a raised bed garden, you will be able to grow plants close to each other when compared to other sectors of gardening. In conventional gardening, the plants are required to be placed at least 3 feet away from each other. This is not the case with raised bed gardening. Always keep a note of the number of plants that you are growing. This is because you will need to harvest them at the right time when they are completely ready. Also, at the time of planting, make sure that you consider the size of the plants. If you are growing tall plants, try to grow them on the northern side of the bed for avoiding casting of shadow on the small-sized plants.

Do not grow plants of various types in one bed. If you are opting for the tier system of growing, you can grow plants of each type in each tier. This will help you to keep the tall plants away from the short plants. It is possible to grow crops of various types in one bed when proper spacing is maintained between the plants in the bed.

Companion Planting

Have you ever come across the phrase 'tomatoes love carrots'? This old saying indicated planting two vegetables that are well-loved together as it can help in improving the yield for both. With the help of companion planting, you can improve the flavor of the produce. There will be less dependency on the chemical-based insecticides and pesticides. As raised bed gardens are efficient, neat, and easy to set up, it can group the plants into a very constrained space. So, choosing the perfect companion for the plants is a very important step for getting the best yield from your crops.

Plants for Repelling Diseases and Pests

There are certain plants that can produce compounds for suppressing the development and growth of other harmful organisms in the garden. Here are some most widely found favorites.

Preferred Crops	Plants For Repelling Pests

Tomatoes	Chives, onions, and garlic can help in preventing the munching pests. Borage helps in repelling tomato hornworms. Asparagus helps in repelling nematodes. Cilantro can be used to prevent spider mites.
Broccoli, Kale, Cabbage	Borage can help in deterring moth caterpillars in cabbages. Garlic can also help in preventing various pests with the help of its sulfur compounds. Marigolds help in deterring maggots.
Potatoes	Catnip can be planted with potatoes for repelling Colorado potato beetle.
Carrots	Clover is planted in carrot growing beds for repelling various types of pests like wireworms. Carrot rust fly can be repelled by growing lettuce, tansy, and basil.
Cucumber	Nasturtiums and onions are planted for attracting important insects that can feed on beetles.

| Squash | Radishes planted with squash plants can repel various types of insects like squash bugs. |

Combination for Improving Flavor

There are various combinations of plants that can be used for improving the flavor of the yield. Let's have a look at them.

- Cilantro or basil planted with tomato
- Chervil planted with radishes
- Chamomile planted with onions

Best Combination for Raised Bed Garden

Onion and garlic planted with tomatoes can help in repelling pests of various types like snails and slugs. Basil grown in the same garden bed of tomatoes can help to improve the flavor of ripe tomatoes. You can plant marigold and radish along with cabbage to control cabbage maggots that tend to attack the roots of cabbage. One of the oldest favorites, called the three sisters, is a combination of squash, corn, and runner beans. Squash can benefit a lot when planted along with beans and corn. Corn also acts as a natural trellis for providing support to the vining beans.

You can plant beets with bush beans and kale. Kale and beans help in adding nutrients to the soil and can be harvested faster than beets. Make sure that you do not plant pole beans with beets as they are not at all compatible with each other. Bean of bush variety is always recommended.

If possible, try to plant flowers in the garden. You can opt for flowers that are edible as they help in improving the flavor of the produce.

Crop Rotation

The overall concept of raised bed gardening is very simple- filling up a frame with soil and then planting crops in the same for years. But, there are certain challenges that are accompanied by the crops in a very restricted area every year. Vegetables, when compared to other types of plants, are more prone to diseases and pests if proper care is not taken. In case pests get entry to the garden bed once, they can multiply very fast. Crop rotation helps a lot in dealing with pests and also helps in bringing back the soil fertility.

Reason for Crop Rotation

- **Prevention of diseases:** The primary reason behind crop rotation is to prevent the spreading of plant diseases. The disease organisms can easily grow over time and thus result in crop failure. As you rotate crops, it helps in keeping a check on such organisms.

- **Soil fertility:** When you keep on growing crops of one type in the same place for a long time, it can degrade soil fertility. Crop rotation helps in replenishing soil fertility by growing crops of various types.
- **Enhancement of nutrients:** Crop rotation helps in enhancing the nutrient content of the soil.

Crop Rotation Principles

The overall concept related to crop rotation depends on the knowledge of the gardener about the plant families of vegetables. It also includes linked quirks and pests. Crop rotation means not cultivating the same or somewhat related kind of crop in the same place for years. This can help in reducing the building up of insects and disease pathogens. Most of the expert growers suggest a rotation cycle of six to seven years. In theory, a garden needs to have a minimum of six to seven beds. You will need to plant each of the beds with a different type of crop every year until the cycle gets completed.

Challenges for Raised Bed Crop Rotation

Specifically, in the small-scale nature of landscapes, having more garden beds is not at all practical. Crop rotation needs to be approached in a creative way in such a case. For many growers, tomatoes are the only reason for cultivating a garden of vegetables. But, the other members of the nightshade group like potatoes, peppers, and eggplant is not possible to be grown in the exact same place every year without resulting in diseases. Soil replacement is a viable option and is expensive as well.

Sample Plan for Planting

With the use of a proper plan and good keeping of record, you can achieve good rotation of crops with as little as four beds only. With every succeeding year, cultivate crops from one bed to the next that is in line. For instance, in a garden with four beds, the first bed can contain onions and spinach during the springtime, tomatoes during summer, and beans at the time of fall. The second bed can hold cabbage, ornamental corn, and beans at the time of fall. The third frame can contain annual rye as the spring cover crop with peppers in summer and garlic at the time of fall. The fourth can contain peas with sweet corn for summer and turnips for the fall.

Supplementing Garden Beds

In all those spaces where having multiple beds is not at all practical, using large-sized containers for growing one plant at a time is the best option. It is a great way for supplementing diversity of the crops. This can help in maintaining the integrity of the crop rotating schedule. There are various types of plants available that are suited for growing in containers.

Tips For Effective Crop Rotation

- Small-sized gardens can be rotated. You can use four areas for planting garden beds.
- Tomatoes and potatoes are closely related to one another. Both are susceptible to diseases of the same kind. That is the reason gardeners group them together. In case you are facing problems with early blight, you will need to separate the two. Make sure that they are placed away from each other.

- As legumes can help in adding nitrogen to the soil, you can follow them by growing leafy crops that love nitrogen. This can help in reducing the need for nitrogen-based fertilizers.
- Root crops tend to break the soil. So, you can follow the growth of root plants with legumes that can help in adding texture to the soil. Also, legumes can grow very well in the soil of loose structure.
- Some vegetables like cucumbers, lettuce, squash, and melons are not much susceptible to diseases. They can be grown almost anywhere or in any kind of space. But, it will be easier for you to plan the garden by rotating and including everything.
- If you have just started with raised bed gardening, you can rotate crops within the number of beds that you have.

Soil

One of the benefits that you can enjoy while growing vegetables in a raised bed is that you can control the quality of the soil. This aspect is of great advantage for all those gardeners who have clay or hard-packed soil, concerns regarding pollutants, or issues with roots of trees. Good quality soil is always regarded as the foundation of a garden that is of a healthy nature. You will want to ensure that vegetables being set up are ready for success only. So, what kind of soil is best suited for raised beds?

You can set up raised beds of any size, but as a standard, the recommended shape is rectangular with about 3 – 4 feet in width and 6 – 8 feet in length with a height of about

10 – 12 inches. All of these dimensions will allow you as a gardener to reach any spot in the bed to sow, plant, and weed without the need to walk on the bed. This results in another benefit when compared to growing crops following the traditional way. The raised bed soil will remain as it is, friable and loose, instead of being packed tight with time because of footsteps. There is no meaning of disturbing the soil quality without any reason.

How Much Soil Is Required?

Filling up a raised bed will need more amount of soil that you actually think. Delivery of soil will make the maximum sense economically. But, if it does not seem practical from the aspect of logistics, you will have to buy it in bags. You will also need to find an area in the yard from where you can take topsoil. You can opt for the various soil calculators that are available online for determining the amount of soil needed for your raised bed.

In case you have cut out sod underneath in the place where you will be setting up the raised bed, flip them, with the grass side down. This will help in filling the bottom part of the bed. You will find lots of soil attached to the grass, and it will break down with time. So, this indicates you need less amount of soil for filling the raised bed. There is no need to use yard soil only. You can get any kind of soil that you think will meet the needs of the crops. Make sure that the topsoil has the highest composition of organic nutrients and matter. Topsoil is the most important layer for a raised bed.

Best Soil for Raised Bed

The most common mix that you can find in the market is the triple mix. It is a great quality mix that comes with compost, topsoil, and black loam or peat moss. A mixture that comes in the ratio of 50/50 is regarded as the perfect blend of soil for raised bed gardens. In the 50/50 mix, you will find a blend of compost and topsoil only. In case you have decided to purchase soil from outside, make sure that you find out where the soil originates from. Topsoil is most often taken from the lands that are being developed for the new subdivisions. It might have been unused for a long period and thus might be devoid of the important nutrients. If you are buying soil bags, look out for labels such as herb mix, organic, vegetable, or organic soil for flowers and vegetables.

No matter what type of soil you purchase, you will need to ensure that you amend the same with proper compost. The rich organic matter acts as an important component that will be holding all the moisture. It will also provide nutrients for the growth of the plants. Compost acts as a very important component in the soil for raised beds, regardless of the mixture of ingredients that you opt for. You can start by filling the raised beds with about ¾ of the triple mix. Even though it comes with compost in it, you can top-dress the soil with ¼ of compost. In case you do not have a compost pile, you can find various types of composts in the market.

Amending Soil Mixture

Both the triple mix and 50/50 mix comes with the basic types of building blocks that you will need for good quality soil in the raised bed. Once you have got the soil of your choice, you can easily amend the soil composition for suiting specific choices of plants. One of the good additions to create well-balanced organic garden soil is slow-releasing organic fertilizer. If you can add this to the soil two to three times in a year, you can easily boost the quality of the soil.

After you have applied it to the soil, do not forget to add compost or mulch for retaining the soil nutrients and moisture. Some other amendments for the soil are:

- Wood chips, shredded bark, or sawdust breaks down at a slow rate and also helps in improving the soil structure.
- You can use used tea bags and coffee grinds for providing the soil with NPK components.
- Dolomite lime can help in improving the soil alkalinity and also adds calcium and magnesium.
- If you want to make the soil well-drained, gypsum can be added.

Mulch helps in holding the soil moisture and also provides protection to the soil from any kind of damage from the sun rays.

Maintenance

Keep removing debris to prevent the development of pests and diseases. Always check for brown edges, wilting, or yellowing in plants. It might be a sign of pest infestation. In such a case, you can use mild insecticide for the soil. Never forget to check the soil condition after a period of heavy rain. You can use a moisture meter to avoid overwatering of soil. Never forget to remove weeds and stalks from the soil. You can also use a pH meter for checking the pH level of the soil.

Planting

Of course, you will not be growing all your vegetables from seeds. You can also opt for readymade plants from the plant nurseries. No matter which route you opt for, this section will be teaching you the various ways of launching your own raised bed garden.

Seeds

Seeds come with great capabilities of producing incredible bounty from the tiny structures. There are various beginner gardeners who regard the starting of seeds warily. But, in actual, seeds are designed a special way in which they can thrive in various conditions and reproduce as time goes on. All that you need to do is to just help them by providing a bit of care. In case you are not willing to start from the seeds, you can opt for transplants. However, seeds do come with certain benefits. They are cheap and many times free. Also, you can find the seeds for rare veggies easily than finding the transplants of the same.

Where to Sow Seeds?

You have got two options for sowing the seeds: in little pots indoors or in the place where you have set up your garden outdoors. You cannot sow seeds of all types of vegetables indoors. Root crops like beets and carrots cannot be disturbed once they have put down roots in the soil. Seeds need warmth, moisture, light, and also oxygen for germination. For sowing seeds, you can use soil that is light and airy in nature. It will provide the seeds with proper air circulation. Maintaining proper moisture might turn out to be a crucial task in the starting. The aim will be to maintain the soil in a state of sponge-damp. Most seeds can germinate when the temperature is maintained between 65 degrees Fahrenheit and 75 degrees Fahrenheit. After the emergence of the seedlings, you will need to provide them with enough light.

Process of Sowing Seeds

Materials needed:

Seeds

Organic mix of soil

Watering can

Trowel

Procedure:

- Start by moistening the bed soil before you sow the seeds. Make sure that the soil is not wet. It needs to be damp. In case you are willing to sow the seeds in containers, this needs to be followed as well.
- Check the packet of seeds for getting information about how deep the seeds need to be sowed in the soil. As a general rule, you can sow seeds at a depth of approximately twice its diameter. So, large-sized seeds, for example, beans, will be sown much deeper than the seeds of carrots. It is better not to sow the seeds too deep as it might make it tough for the seeds to reach the surface of the soil.
- If you are sowing large seeds, use a pencil or chopstick and a poke a small hole in the soil. Place the seed in the hole and cover the hole with soil. For the seeds of small size, you can just sprinkle them on the soil top and just cover them with a light layer of soil. If you are willing to sow many seeds at one time, create a trench of shallow nature with the trowel edge. You can scatter the seeds or place them along the created trench.

- You will need to follow the spacing guidelines along with the direction that has been provided with the seed packet.
- In case you are sowing more than one type of seed, make sure that you mark the area of the seeds.
- Some seeds can germinate within two to three days, while some might take weeks.
- You will need to keep the soil moist all throughout the period of sprouting and germination.

Planting Seedlings

- If the seedlings have been grown in peat pots, you will need to remove the pots and then place the seedlings in the holes prepared by you.
- If you have grown seedlings in plastic pots, make sure that you scrape the base of the seedling properly along with the soil.
- You will need to plant seedlings at the same depth as they were sowed in the growing pots. If you tend to sow them deeper, the plant might fail to breathe.

Planting Seeds in Block

- Start by outlining the blocks with the help of a shallow trench or furrow.
- Lay down tape measure through the block sides to ensure proper spacing of the seeds.
- Try to maintain a gap of 3 inches.
- Start with 3 inches, followed by 6 inches, and so on for your first row.
- For planting the next section, move the measuring tape 3 inches back. Keep on doing this until you have filled up the block.

- After you are done with this, cover the seeds with the help of soil.

Growing and Harvesting

Growing and harvesting are not much tougher in a raised bed garden. You will need to follow certain tips and suggestions for getting the best out of your raised bed.

Watering

No matter which type of system you choose for watering your garden, you will need to pay proper attention at the time of its operation.

Paying Attention to Weather

Plants will need more water when the conditions are windy and dry. During extreme heat, raised bed gardens might require daily watering. During other times of the year, you can water the garden only 2 – 3 times a week.

Being Aware of the Watering Needs

Make sure that you monitor the signs of stress that might result from under watering of the plants. If you have plants in the garden that are wilting during the afternoon but recovers by the morning are suffering from the stress of heat and not water. You will need to permit the growing plants to develop some tolerance to heat by not watering them excessively. Signs of plant over-watering include rotten roots, soft roots, constant wet soil, and leaf drop.

Water During Morning

Plants tend to absorb moisture in an effective way during the morning. As you water the plants early, it can help in hydrating the plants before the heat of the daytime. Morning plant watering also helps in preventing waterborne pests. It can also deal with diseases of various kinds that might occur in case you water plants at night.

Thinning and Feeding Seedlings

A plant's cotyledon or leaves are the first to develop from the soil. These emerging leaves provide the plant with all the required nutrition until the emergence of true leaves. So, after the appearance of the true leaves, you will need to feed the seedlings every week with a combo of liquid emulsion. In case you want to add a little bit of compost or castings of worms to the mix of seed-starting, this step can be skipped.

During this stage, you will need to make several tough decisions regarding what you want to do with the new seedlings. You will need to keep them free to provide room for breathing. So, you will need to thin out the seedlings, cutting down the weakest one at the level of the soil. Your aim will be to leave one seedling every 3 inches. In case you thin the final space at an early stage, you will end up winding with fewer numbers of plants than you actually intended to.

Mulching

You will need to take care of mulching while growing plants in raised beds. It is very important as it helps in retaining soil moisture, deters weeds, and also helps in regulating soil temperature. You can mulch at layers by using four inches of straw mulch or shredded leaves.

Fertilizing

Timing is the key to effective fertilization of vegetables. Young plants, specifically peppers, and tomatoes might find it tough to adjust to outdoor life. So, if you apply fertilizer at an early stage, the tender plant roots might get burnt. Fertilizers come with varying nutrient composition for the plants. You will need to ensure the requirements of the plants in your garden before opting for a fertilizer.

Harvesting

Harvesting can be done best during the morning. You will need to check the garden plants daily for any kind of issues and also look out for the produce that is ready for harvesting. For example, corn needs to be harvested when the cobs start swelling with the tassels turning brown in color. Harvesting of herbs and leafy vegetables can be done according to your preference. For tomatoes, the perfect time for harvesting will be when the tomatoes are red in color and firm. In case you are willing to grow tomato of some other color, you will need to wait for the same.

Weeding

Weeding is an important part of raised bed gardening. The task of weeding will be easier for you during the morning as the watering or dew can help in making the soil loose. If you break up and loosen the soil regularly, it can discourage the growth of weed. In case weed develops, try to pull them out from the roots as much as you can. You can cover the garden with a layer of plastic mulch or cardboard. It will help in minimizing weed growth between the final harvest and the upcoming season of growing. Also, make sure that you clean the garden by removing dead leaves and decaying debris.

Pest Control

Dealing with the problems of diseases and pests is a natural part of gardening. Well, it might feel really disturbing when pests attack the garden at the time of harvesting or when the plants are growing. Insecticides can be used or dealing with them. But, insecticides can effectively alter the pH level of the soil and can also introduce chemical components to the garden. So, it is better to keep them away as much as you can. There are certain ways in which you can control pests without the use of insecticides.

- Try to maintain healthy soil. A healthy type of soil can help in developing a strong immune system for the plants so that they can fight with diseases and pests. In case you want to use fertilizer of any kind, opt for the organic one.
- Choose plant varieties that are resistant to pests. This is one of the easiest ways of dealing with pests. For instance, the tromboncino variety of squash is more pest-resistant than other varieties of summer squash.
- Try to provide the plants with the required supplies. When the plants are deprived of something, they will tend to get weak and can easily attract pests.
- There are various beneficial insects that can eat away pests. Such insects can be attracted to the garden with the use of pollen and nectar. You can also introduce pest eating bugs like ladybugs and lacewings.

- You can plant strong-scented herbs that can help in deterring pests. This is an easy way of keeping away pests from the garden. Some example of strong-scented plants is garlic, calendula, and coriander.
- Crop rotation can help in dealing with pests. It can also help in managing the fertility of the garden soil. You will need to leave a gap of one to two years before planting crops of the same type in a particular area. It might turn out to be a challenge for small spaces, but if a plant gets infested by pests, try not to grow that type of plant in the same area for the next two to three years.
- You can try out interplanting for dealing with pests. It means growing alternate crops between herbs, vegetables, and flowers. Instead of practicing monocropping, try to alternate the row of veggies with beneficial insect attracting plants and flowers that can repel pests.
- In case you notice pest infestation, try to remove them manually. If a plant gets infested by pests, removing that plant from the garden will be the best option. You can use mild insecticides of organic nature in case the infestation spreads rapidly. You can spray neem oil for keeping away pests.

CHAPTER 2

Container Gardening

Tubs, pots, and half barrels overfilled with vegetables and flowers can easily add appeal to a garden of any kind. But, other than improving the look of a garden, container gardening can serve certain practical purposes as well. Container gardening is a perfect choice for all those people who have no or very little space for gardening. Along with growing flowers, gardeners who are limited to a small yard, balcony, or a little patch of sunlight on the driveway can grow various types of vegetables in containers. Herbs such as chives, thyme, and basil can grow quite happily in containers. Thus they can be set in a little spot outside your kitchen area.

Container gardening adds versatility to gardens of both small and large sizes. As you opt for container gardening, you can add instant colors to the garden and add a focal point for the garden. Either place the containers on a pedestal or the ground, hang them from the porch, or mount them on the windowsill. A container garden can help in improving the look of your house from all possible angles. You can pair matching containers by the sides of the front walk for creating a welcoming décor. Container garden on patio or deck can add ambiance and color to your outdoor area of sitting.

You have the option of using large and single containers for decorating outside. But, you can also consider arranging the containers or pots in groups, both large and small, on terraces, stairways, or in any other place in the garden. Pot clusters can contain a wide variety of your favorite plants, herbs, veggies, and flowers. They can also contain dwarf evergreens and perennials that you would like to try. You can also use hanging baskets and window boxes for adding instant appeal and color to your house.

In most of the cases, plants of only one species are grown in containers. But, you can grow two to three species of plants in large containers. Always keep one thing in mind; it is easier to grow your plants in large-sized containers when compared to the small ones. The main reason behind this is large containers can hold more amount of soil. So, they can stay moist for a longer period. Also, large containers can prevent the rapid fluctuation of temperature. The small baskets are most likely to get dried out, and you will need to water the containers two to three times during very hot weather.

Another thing that you will need to keep in mind is to determine the type of plants that you are willing to grow in the containers. There are various factors that can help you in determining how deep and large the containers need to be. Before you opt for a container, try to consider the shape and size of the root system of the plants that you will be growing. The rate at which the plants grow is another factor that you will need to keep in mind. The rootbound plants that come with the tendency of covering every inch of the available soil dry out faster. They won't be able to grow cells. In case you are willing to grow plants of various types in one container, you will need to use large containers for providing enough root space for the growing plants.

The maximum size of a pot or container will depend on the space that you are having, the plants that will be grown in it, and whether you will be moving the same in the future. Just like other types of gardens, container gardening also needs certain basic elements such as oxygen, water, sun, nutrients, etc. You can make a checklist for ticking off the important requirements of plants as you plan to grow them in containers.

Let us start with the basics of container gardening, and we will progress slowly to the other aspects.

Basics

Plants cannot be grown when certain elements are not present, such as water, nutrients, sunlight, drainage, etc. Container gardening is similar to the other sectors of gardening, and it also needs the basic elements of growing.

Sun

Plants grown in containers need sunlight, but the amount of required sunlight will vary from one plant to the other. Vegetables that are grown for the seeds or fruits, such as peppers, tomatoes, cucumber, and eggplant, requires almost 6 – 8 hours of sunlight that is of direct nature every day. Ideally, this can be from dawn till about 3 pm. The sunlight tends to be the hottest after three in the afternoon till sundown. Leafy vegetables such as lettuce, Swiss chard, cabbage, and spinach can grow in less amount of sunlight. Plants like the culinary herbs and flowering houseplants might come with varying requirements of light.

As you decide to grow plants of a certain kind, make sure that you check the labels of seed packets. This needs to be done to find the ideal requirement of sunlight. You will need to get familiar with the amount of sun that is received by a certain spot of gardening. If possible, you can imagine the altering exposure of sunlight as the plants grow leaves and as the seasons keep in changing. For the productive nature of container gardening, it is better not to combine plants that require a varying amount of sunlight. This needs to be followed if you are growing various containers in one single spot or several plants in one pot or container.

The primary advantage of container gardening that it has over the traditional form of soil gardening is that the containers can be moved. In case you find out that the plants are not at all happy with the amount of sun being received, you can easily pick up the containers and place them in some other spot that comes with better conditions for the plants. If you are new to the world of container gardening, it will be better for you if you opt for the native plants of your area. Native plants will be adjusted to the growing conditions of your area. Thus, it will be able to adapt to the local climate and lighting changes. It will be easier for you to maintain such plants.

Almost all types of plants can be grown in container gardening. But, one thing that you will need to remember is that container gardening will not be altering the basic needs of the plants. Plants that are sun-loving will require lots of sunlight. The shade-loving plants will grow their best when kept under dappled light.

Drainage

No matter what type of plant you decide to grow in container gardening, drainage holes are very important. Without the presence of proper drainage, the soil in the container will tend to be waterlogged. It will eventually result in dying plants. The holes are not required to be very large but should be enough to allow the excess water to drain out of the container. In case containers come with no holes for drainage, you can drill some according to your need. Containers that come with no holes are used as a cachepot for hiding plain pots. Cachepots are very useful in managing heavy pots and large plants. You can grow plants in any ordinary pot that sits inside cachepot so that you can move the pots separately.

You can also opt for self-watering containers, hanging baskets, window boxes, and double-walled containers. These options can be helpful for dealing with plants that are of small size and need frequent watering. If you try to omit drainage in containers, you will be leaving the garden at high risk. Plants need water, light, and air to deal with their life in containers. Plant roots require water to deal with chemical processes of all kinds. It is also needed for transporting nutrients to the plants from the soil. Roots need air as well. In case the root systems of plants are left with no oxygen for a long period, the roots will suffocate. Thus, resulting in dead plants. Also, when you have excessive water near the root area, it can easily inhibit the availability of air.

Things turn out to be more complicated when you grow plants in containers. So, you will need to look after the drainage for ensuring adequate escaping of extra water. Proper drainage can help in improving the container soil structure, increases the effectiveness of phosphorus-based fertilizers, and conserves nitrogen. It also helps in preventing leaching and waterlogging.

Also, excessive drainage is not suitable for plants. In case you are experiencing excessive water drainage from the containers, you will need to water the plants more frequently. In case you fail to water the plants quickly, plants will dry out and will die. The main reason behind the problem of this kind could be container soil. It can happen if the soil is having an extreme proportion of sandy soil. Sandy soil cannot retain water effectively. On the contrary, if the soil is clayey, it might result in water stagnation. In such a case, it might result in root rot. The best solution for the problem of this kind is to add compost to the container soil before growing plants.

You can also opt for improving the soil structure to deal with drainage problems. You can add gravel or sand to improve the structure. You can also add rocks at the base of containers. This can be done with containers with holes and the ones that do not come with holes of any kind. In this case, the rocks at the base act like a reservoir, storing all the excess amount of water until the same get drawn up by the roots. For the containers with holes, the rock bed allows flowing out of excess water while preventing the soil particles and dirt from escaping. You can use gravels made from pebbles or granite. This is a very popular technique that is being used for container gardening by most gardeners.

Water

It is actually a tough job to determine the amount of water that is needed by container plants. A very fine line exists between soggy soil and drought soil, and either of the two can be dangerous for plant health. Summer is considered the toughest time for watering container plants. You can use a moisture gauge for easing your job of watering plants. Container plants have the tendency of drying out quickly when compared to the in-ground plants. The small amount of soil space, along with the container construction, can store a minimal amount of moisture. Generally, watering plants early in the morning or in the evening is considered the perfect time. This helps the plants to take in more amount of water before the day heat. It will also allow the plants to evaporate excess water. Thus the plants will not be vulnerable to any kind of fungus.

You will need to water the plants when the soil is dry, and that is a very common thing to do. But, only watering when the soil dries up might not be a good thing for the plants. Try to look out for limp stems, shriveled leaves, discolored leaves, and dropping petals. These are the signs of water deficiency. You will need to check the container plants daily in dry and warm conditions. Usually, when the top inch of the soil is dry, it is a good time to water the plants. You might need to water the plants twice in a day when the temperature goes above 85 degrees Fahrenheit.

If you are checking the containers all the time, you will know exactly when to water the plants. The frequency of watering will depend on the species and type of plant that you are growing. The drought-tolerant and succulent plants will need to be watered much less when compared to the annuals. The well-established plants can thrive longer without water than the plants that are newly installed. While watering the container plants, make sure that you water slowly so that the water can be accessed by every part of the root and soil. Light and short watering is most likely to get drained out of the holes much before the plants can actually take in some of the moisture. In fact, the majority of the container soil will start repelling water if left dried out for a long period. As you water deep and slow, it will ensure that the water reaches the roots of the plants. It will also force the dried soil to start absorbing water again.

In case the container soil has been completely dried out, it will be wise of you to soak the containers completely in a tub full of water. Soak the container for about 30 minutes or so for forcing rehydration of the soil. The amount of water that you will need to provide to the plants will vary greatly from one plant to the other. You can determine the average requirement of moisture of any specific plant and then get into use a moisture gauge. You will need to stick the gauge probe in the soil that will give you a reading about the level of moisture in the soil. If the container plants need moderately wet soil and the gauge shows readings in dry zones, you will need to water the plants. You can use glazed containers for preventing evaporation of water from the walls.

Tip: Water the plants when the temperature is cooler.

Logistics

Container gardening can be done anywhere without any kind of restriction. The best aspect of container gardening is that you can move the containers anywhere and anytime you want. It would be great if you can set up container gardening in the balcony, terrace, stairways, or even in your yard at a corner. Make sure that you do not keep containers on the sidewalk or near the entry gate. You can arrange the containers in benches by a corner to make the best out of the space you have.

While planning out the garden, make sure that you do not place the containers in spots that are prone to pests. You can move the containers anytime you want. Still, it is always better to prevent the onset of pests for avoiding future hassle. You can use hanging baskets for making use of the windowsill. The front yard can also be used, and in that case, you can place the containers close to a watering source.

Size

Growing your own vegetables in containers is a very popular and easy way of experiencing the flavors along with the freshness of homegrown crops. Here's a very well-known secret: most types of vegetables can grow very well in pots and containers. By choosing the perfect plants, you can easily create a small container vegetable garden and grow a decent amount of food within a few containers only.

But why give in the extra effort of growing veggies in containers rather than buying them from the market? Well, with the help of a container vegetable garden, you will be able to grow vegetables that you might not find in the market. Growing vegetables in containers is much easier than you think. Let's have a look at the perfect types and sizes of containers suited for your vegetable garden.

Types of Containers

Not sure what type of container to opt for your vegetable garden? It is not a problem at all as vegetables are not that fussy about the type of containers that they are grown in. The one and the only requirement for containers of a vegetable garden is that they need to be large enough for holding the plants. It should also have holes from drainage so that the extra amount of water can easily escape. Vegetables that are grown in clay containers are needed to be taken extra care of when compared to plants of other types. This is mainly because clay containers are porous in nature and can give out a lot of water via evaporation. You will need to pay attention to the color of the container as well. Do not opt for containers that are made out of treated wood as the chemicals can disturb the growth of the plants.

While talking about the size of the garden, there is no limit as such. The size of a container vegetable garden will depend solely on the size of the containers that are being used. But, keep one thing in mind, the bigger the container, the better will be the growth. This aspect works best for beginner gardeners. The main reason behind this is that large containers can hold more amount of soil. So, it can retain moisture for a longer period. So, you will not need to water the plants frequently. You can opt for vegetable growing containers that are 10 inches in width and 12 inches in depth. This is the ideal container size for beginners. Large-sized flower pots, window boxes, and large-sized containers of about 5 gallons will also work fine.

Certain vegetables need large pots for growing properly in a container garden. Tomatoes of standard size and vining veggies like cucumber can be grown the best in containers that are of 25 inches or even more across. Peppers can be grown, preferably in pots that are minimum 15 inches in diameter. However, vegetables of all size can be grown in containers of large size. Plants such as cucumber and tomato have the tendency to grow tall. They will produce vines that will be grown the best when provided with support in container gardening. You can use a wire cage that needs to be installed at the time of planting can provide the required support. You will need to use large and heavy containers for the trellised nature of plants. This needs to be done to minimize the overall risk of tipping.

Building Structures and Designs

In container gardening, everything is done in containers. So, there is no need for building any extra structure as the concept of container gardening moves around the easy movement of containers and plants. As there are is nothing like building structures in container gardening, we will be discussing the various types of container garden designs in this section.

Similar to decorating your home, a good decoration of containers is also a matter of self aesthetics. There will be several combinations of colors that will be appealing, while others will not. The secret to a great container design is to find out what your choice is and what you love. However, good designing of container gardening goes much beyond the choice of colors. It is more about partnering textures and pairing veggies and herbs in a pleasing manner. It is all about combining the perfect veggies with the perfect containers.

Proportion

Plantings that are not in proper proportion with the containers will tend to look top-heavy, flat, too dense, or not at all appealing depending on the design of the gardener. Design is important even if your goal is to set up a natural looking container garden and nothing that looks planned. You can start by looking at the container height. For proper proportion, the container that you have chosen needs to comprise of either 1/2 or 2/3 of the overall height of the container and plants combined. In simple terms, you need to aim for a ratio of 2:1 or 1:2. You will not be able to establish proper proportions until the appropriate height of the plants is reached.

Focal Point

Another vital point for container gardening design is to have one focal point. Many times the largest type of plant tends to be the focal point naturally because of its size. But, you can base the focal point of your garden on bold structures of a leaf, jazzy color, and vertical element. Try to keep only one focal point for each of the containers in the garden.

Designing With the Help of Edible Plants

Veggies and fruits are often cultivated in a utilitarian manner. Minimal thought is given to the layout and design of the container. There are various gardeners who love to focus on the productivity of the garden and not the layout and design of the container. But, you can actually do both great looking and highly productive garden in containers. The vessels containing vegetables can also be turned into something beautiful. There is no need for plunking the tomato plants in one large container all for themselves. You can grow tomatoes in the middle of a large container. It can be surrounded by herbs and short vegetable plants like peppers. You can also opt for spinach and lettuce for filling up the soil bed by the sides. Another great combination is to grow root crops like beets and carrots in the middle with sweet potatoes or cherry tomatoes by the sides. The design is all up to you. Just focus on not making the containers look clumsy.

Plants

Container gardening is a very effective way of saving space and growing fresh vegetables in any corner of your house. As you grow veggies in containers, you can easily deal with diseases and pests. Also, it takes much less time for growing plants than the conventional type of garden. You can also group plants that can help each other in containers. This technique is called companion planting. It will be easier for you to maintain the quality of plants as the allocated space is quite small.

Plant Journal

A plant journal can be maintained for keeping track of the plants that you have grown. It can help you maintain a record of the needs of the plants. Always keep in mind that you will need to mention the time of harvesting so that you can omit that plant for one or two years for effective crop rotation. It will be discussed in the later sections.

Spacing

You will need to provide the vegetable plants appropriate space for maturing. When you provide proper spacing to the plants, the roots of the plants will not need to compete with each other for moisture and nutrients. Also, proper spacing can ensure the right exposure of light to the plant surface that is required for growth. It also helps in proper air circulation. You can grow root and leafy vegetables in the containers with the use of seeds. But, once they grow in size, you will need to thin them. Crops that provide fruits like peppers and tomatoes can provide the best produce when started in small pots of 3 – 4 inches and alter transplanted to large containers.

As you provide proper spacing to the plants, it will be easier for you to apply fertilizer to the plants. Also, the spreading of pests can be minimized.

Plants Suitable for Container Gardening

Various types of vegetables can be grown in containers. Let's have a look at them.

Beans

Green beans can be grown in containers and can act as a great addition to your courtyard or balcony. There are two proper ways of growing beans using containers. You can opt for the bush variety of beans that can grow very happily in containers without the need for any kind of support. The second one is the climbing variety and needs trellis for support. You can opt for the second option for making the best use of the vertical space as it is possible to run them on the fences and walls. Beans of any type need a minimum depth of 12 inches.

Beets

Beets are a great option for growing in confined spaces. The only aspect that you will need to focus on is to provide them with deep containers for proper development of the roots. You can pick a container of 12 -14 inches in depth for growing beet. You can grow various types of beets in containers such as Chioggia. This variety of beet comes with candy stripes with alternating white and red rings.

Chard

If a competition is conducted for finding the best-suited vegetables to be grown in containers, nothing can beat lettuces and leafy vegetables. Productive and fast-growing, this undisputed king of the world of edible plants makes a great choice as a potted crop. Lettuces and leafy green vegetables hardly need any space for thriving and come with a shallow root system.

Peppers

They are perfect for making the best use of small garden space. All that they need is a warm and sunny place for growing. You will need to provide them with a minimum container depth of 10 inches.

Companion Planting

There are various plants that can be grown together to help each other.

Salad Mix

You can grow a mix of salad vegetables that will be helpful for your cooking and also beneficial for the related plants. In a container of large size, you can grow tomato about 4 inches from the back of the container. As the plants mature, it won't shade the small plants. You can grow a combination of spinach and lettuce around the tomato plants. Sprinkle some seeds of carrots along the outer border of the container. Make sure that the arrangement you are going to make can provide room for the growth of individual plants. In case you want to aid the container from pests and insects, plant rosemary and sage by the sides.

Root Vegetables

Plant lettuce between various types of root crops like turnips, onions, beets, and carrots. It can help to retain the moisture of the soil and can also provide the soil with proper shade. Lettuce tends to grow very fast and can be harvested much before the growth of the root vegetables. So, plants in this type of combination can be grown close to each other for maximizing the available space. You can plant the root vegetables at the indicated distance on the pack of seeds and plant the seeds of lettuce in between. When any of the root crops mature, its foliage will provide shade to the soil when you start harvesting the lettuce.

Tomatoes

If you want to grow tomatoes in your garden, you can dedicate some of the containers for growing tomatoes along with their companions. In each of the tomato containers, plant chives or onions spaced narrowly in rows with the growth of carrots. You can grow cucumber with support along with tomatoes. You can also include few clumps of parsley along the corners of the containers. Marigold can be used as a border for repelling insects.

Squash and Beans

If you are willing to fill the garden with summer veggies, you can interplant beans with squash. Marigold can also be used for repelling insects. However, both beans and squash can grow in bush or vining form. You will need to grow either of the two in alteration of the other variety. For example, if you are growing beans of vining variety, you will need to grow squash of bush variety and vice versa. This way, either of the plants will be staying low and will shade the soil.

Crop Rotation

Crop rotation is all about moving vegetables all around the garden to maintain the fertility of the soil. In the case of container gardening, you can rotate crops among containers. As you rotate crops from one place to the other in the same season or the other, you will be able to preserve the nutrients of the soil. Some vegetables are heavy feeders like broccoli, tomatoes, cabbage, eggplant, corn, beets, and leafy vegetables. Light feeders include sweet potato, onions, garlic, peppers, radish, potato, and turnips. Soil builders include beans and peas. As you rotate these three groups of vegetables every season, you can make the best use of the soil nutrients.

Simple Rotation of Crops

This process includes planting heavy feeders in a container for the first year, followed by the group of light feeders the second year. The soil builders will be planted in the third year. This way, you will be able to preserve the quality of the soil and also grow vegetables of various types.

Rotating crops in containers might turn out to be a tough job if you have only a few containers. In such a case, you will still be able to opt for crop rotation. You can grow beans right after growing tomatoes. You can also replace a heavy feeding vegetable such as cabbage in the spring, peas in the fall, and beans in the next year.

Rotating Crops According to Harvest Groups

This is a very simple strategy for crop rotation. It includes rotating root crops, leafy crops, and fruiting crops. You can follow a simple crop rotation plan for three years divided into separate groups of harvesting.

- Leafy crops: Spinach, lettuce, and other members of the cabbage family like cauliflower, broccoli, and Brussels sprouts.
- Root crops: Potatoes, carrots, parsnips, and turnips.
- Fruiting crops: Peppers, tomatoes, cucumbers, eggplants, and squash.

In this mix, you can also add cover crops for following the fruiting crops. As most of the fruiting crops are grown during the summer – peppers, tomatoes, melons, squash, eggplants, they can be harvested during early autumn. So, the planting area of such crops can be used for replanting with winter cover crops like fava beans and winter rye. In the spring, the cover crop can be turned under, and you can grow leafy crops for continuing the crop rotation. The rotation will look like:

- Fruiting crop
- Cover crop
- Root crop
- Leafy crop

Crop Rotation With Plant Family

This is the traditional way of rotating crops, and it might be a bit tough for container gardening. In this method, crops that belong to the same family are not grown in the same container for over three to four years. It not only helps in maintaining the fertility of the soil but also acts as a great process for keeping away diseases and pests. If you tend to grow crops of the same family consecutively, pests and diseases will be more prone to them. Some of the notable plant families of vegetables that can be used for crop rotation in container gardening are:

- Squash family: Winter squash, cucumber, zucchini, melons

- Tomato family: Tomato, pepper, eggplant
- Cabbage family: Broccoli, cabbage, arugula, kale, collards
- Lettuce family: Artichokes, endive, sunchokes
- Bean family: Peas and beans
- Spinach family: Spinach, beet, sweet chard
- Onion family: Shallots, onion, leeks
- Carrot Family: Parsley, celery, parsnips, cilantro, fennel

Soil

Choosing soil for container gardening is not that difficult. But, the primary drawback that comes with container gardening is that the soil in the containers cannot be regenerated. They cannot gain extra nutrients from mother earth. The root system in container gardening cannot grow much deep into the soil. Plants that are grown in containers depend entirely on the growers for providing them with all that they need to survive. That is why you are required to choose the soil for container gardening properly. But how will you know which variety of soil will be the best for your garden? This section will be discussing various tips and suggestions for choosing the perfect soil for container gardening and which one to avoid.

Choosing Soil for Potting

Soil is regarded as the foundation for growing healthy plants. So, you will need to ensure that you use soil that is of high quality for growing plants in containers. When you start with a good mix of soil, you will be able to grow better quality plants. Good soil mix is expensive, indeed, but that is what will make all the difference. There are various types of soil that you will come across if you ever visit a local plant nursery. Soil also comes with a lot of dirt, and those are not at all suitable for growing plants in containers. Many beginner gardeners make the mistake of using soil from their garden or yard in the containers. You can grow plants using soil from the garden, but you will be actually taking a huge risk. First of all, soil from the garden is most likely to have nasty stuff like insects and bugs, weed seeds, disease organisms, etc. If you try using soil of this kind, you will be destroying your container garden with your own hands.

Secondly, garden soil is heavy in nature to be used for container gardening. It will tend to get compact very easily after a few days. In that case, plants will find it really difficult to grow in containers. So, it is always suggested not to opt for garden soil for containers and use only potting soil for ensuring the growth of the plants.

Best Soil for Gardening in Containers

It is important to choose soil of the best quality for container plants, but it is not required to be intimidating at all. If you are buying soil from outside, make sure that you check the label on it if it has been created for a certain purpose. For the majority of the outdoor plants, opting for an all-purpose mix of soil for container gardening is regarded as the best option. You can also choose soil by checking the consistency of the same. Here are some of the important things that you will need to look for a quality mix of soil.

- The soil is fluffy and light.
- The soil has good drainage. Make sure it can retain moisture that is needed.

- It is porous in nature so that air and water can reach the system of roots easily.
- There is no form of weed seed in the soil bag or any kind of tiny bugs.
- Make sure sand is not mixed with the soil.
- It needs to be moist in nature but not soggy. The smell needs to be pleasant.

Soil for Large Containers

Before opting for the type of soil that you will be using for container gardening, determine where you would like to place the plants. A mix of compost and soil will be heavier and is perfect for large containers. You will not need to think about the weight of the container as it will be sitting on the ground. So, you can opt for an all-purpose soil mix for large containers.

Soil for Hanging Baskets

When you decide to grow plants in hanging baskets, you will need to think about the container weight. You cannot make the basket too heavy with soil and water as it will be hanging. So, for hanging baskets, you can use a potting mix that is soilless. Soilless mixtures are made with coco coir or peat moss as the basic ingredient and are light in weight. Also, they do not come with sand or compost.

Reusing Container Soil

If you are trying to reuse container soil, you will be making a huge mistake. It might get contaminated with bugs and diseases from the last cultivation and can infect the new plants. Also, the soil will be having zero nutrients left as it will be used by the last grown plants. So, it will be better for you if you can dump used soil and start again with fresh soil. This way, you can ensure the proper growth of plants. But, if you have very deep containers, there is no need to replace the soil. You will need to remove above 4 – 5 inches of the topsoil and replace it with fresh soil before you start planting new crops. The soil amount that will be needed will depend on the size of the container that you will be using for growing plants. It can also vary according to the size and number of plants.

Before you fill soil in containers, make sure that the containers are clean. If you fill soil in dirty containers, it might result in an infestation of pests and diseases.

Planting

There are various vegetables that can grow the best in containers. Such vegetables include root vegetables, leafy vegetables, warm-season vegetables, and so on. In case you want to grow vegetables from transplants, you can do that. But, in container gardening, it is always suggested to grow vegetables from seeds.

Sowing Seeds

Many plants can start off better when grown in containers. You can even grow super fine seeds that cannot be grown using traditional methods. When containers are provided with adequate light and warm temperatures, the growth rate of plants can easily be improved. Make sure that you check all the information on the seed packet before sowing them in containers. You will get all the required information regarding watering and spacing on the seed packets. Before you sow the seeds, you will need to choose the type of container first in which you will be growing the plants. Cost, convenience, and reusability will be determining the type of container that you can use for sowing seeds. In case you are not able to water the garden daily, it will be better for you to opt for containers of 3 – 4 inches in diameter.

Plastic flats are the most widely used type of container that comes with no dividers at all. You can get them easily from any local gardening store. Sometimes you might even get them for free when you buy seeds. Next comes peat pots that are cheap but cannot be reused. The best aspect of the peat pot is that it minimizes the overall disturbance to the root system at the time of transplantation. But, you will need to keep them moist most of the time. You can also use plastic flats made from foam that has tapered cells. You can get them in various sizes, and some also come with capillary matting for drawing water from the soil. This can make the task of caring for the seedlings easier.

In addition to all the types of containers mentioned above, you can use items from your household as well, such as plastic cups, milk cartons, and so on. In case you are growing the seeds in this type of container, you will need to punch some holes at the base for ensuring proper drainage. You can sow the seeds directly in large containers, but make sure that you mark the spots if you are growing several types of plants at one time.

Process of Sowing Seeds

Materials Needed:

Soil Mix

Seeds

Container

Watering Can

Trowel

Procedure:

- You can start with your own soil mixture. You can also get soil mix from the garden stores that come with a combination of various essential elements. In case you want to make your own soil mix, mix peat moss, perlite, and vermiculite with soil from your garden.
- Dampen the soil mix before you fill-up the containers.
- Fill the containers up to the rim, leaving about ½ inch gap from the top. Firm the soil mix with your fingers.
- Check the information on the seed packet for the recommended depth of planting the seeds.
- You can either make furrows in the container with the help of trowel or simply scatter the seeds on the top of the soil.
- After you are done with scattering or sowing the seeds, you will need to cover the seeds with a fine layer of soil mix.
- If you are using individual pots for the individual types of seeds, you can label them. Mention the date of sowing to keep a record of the germination time.

- In case you are using small containers, you will have to cover the containers with damp newspaper. This will help in keeping the container soil moist for a long period while allowing air through it.
- Place the containers with sowed seeds in a warm spot for speedy germination.
- Ensure that you do not sow the seeds too deep; otherwise, the seeds will not be able to breathe.

Growing and Harvesting

Growing and harvesting in a container garden is not a tough job. But, there are certain aspects that you will need to take care of for ensuring the proper growth of plants.

Watering

Growing plants in containers come along with various benefits, but there are certain challenges as well. One of such challenges is correct watering. Proper watering is very important for the health of growing plants. While the majority of the people tend to get worried about under-watering of plants but in actual it is similarly easy to overwater the plants. As you over water the plants, you will bed drowning them. Make sure that the soil in the garden is moist and not soggy. However, different plants come with different requirements of moisture. There are certain plants that like to be dry, while some like to be a bit moist all the time. Juicy vegetables such as melons, cucumbers, and tomatoes like to be moist and thus needs a great amount of water. Herbs such as cilantro, basil, and thyme like to be in the middle, not too moist and not too dry. You will need to keep a regular tab on the requirements of your plants.

Before you water the plants, always check if the plants actually need watering. In most of the cases, the topsoil might feel dry, but it can be moist underneath. The easiest way of checking whether you need to water the plants is to stick your finger into the soil. If your fingertips feel dry, you will need to water the plants. If it feels moist, there is no need for watering the plants. The level of moisture can change very fast during hot and sunny days. So, a container that feels moist during the day might get dry by the afternoon.

When you water the plants, make sure that you give the plants a slow and long drink. Look for water coming out of the drainage holes at the base of the container. When you see water coming out of the holes, it means water has gone down to the base of the root tips which is required for the plants. Try to opt for shallow and frequent watering for making the roots of the plants to be at the top of the containers. This needs to be done in areas of drought and heat.

Plant roots tend to be more receptive to water during the morning and in the evening. So, whenever you decide to water the plants, make sure it is in the morning or in the evening. Out of the two options of watering the plants, watering during the morning is a better option. Watering during the evening will allow water to settle on the leaves, and this might result in fungal diseases like powdery mildew. Always note that you will need to water the soil and not the leaves. In case you water the leaves, the leaves might get sunburns. The droplets of water will act like small magnifying glasses and will burn the plant.

Even when you think that rainwater has watered the container plants properly, it is better to check the soil. Sometimes the foliage of plants and the flowers might act as umbrellas and can prevent the water from reaching the soil. In case you let the soil mix to get dry completely, it might stop absorbing water. If the soil gets dried out completely, poke holes on the soil surface, and give it a long and good drink. You might also need to water the plants more than once if the weather becomes too hot and dry. But, if you see wilting of plants during the day, do not opt for watering the plants immediately. Sometimes it might happen that the soil is moist and the plants still wilt. In such a case, the plants will get back to its normal state once the sun gets down.

Thinning

Growing vegetables using seeds is cheaper than using seedlings. But, it does involve some extra work. Many gardeners have the tendency to plant seeds of vegetables by sprinkling them in rows. As the seeds germinate, the seedlings are most likely to be spaced very close to one another. So, you will need to pluck the seedlings systematically for providing the other seedlings with the required room to grow. As you thin seedlings in container gardening, you will be able to produce healthy plants. You can have more yields simply by reducing the overall competition for getting nutrients and water from the soil. The plants will also be able to get better circulation of air.

You can thin the seedlings when they produce two to three leaves. Wait for the leaves to get about 3 inches tall for making the pulling task easier for you. In case you like to pull out the seedlings rather than cutting them with a scissor, thinning when the soil is moist and dry will make the whole task a lot easy for you. Every vegetable comes with its desired spacing.

- Carrots: 3 – 4 inches
- Beets: 3 – 5 inches
- Onions: 3 – 5 inches
- Lettuce: 15 – 18 inches
- Spinach: 3 – 6 inches
- Radishes: 3 – 4 inches
- Turnips: 3 – 4 inches
- Parsnips: 4 – 6 inches

Seedlings that are started from pots will not need thinning as you will be able to separate them at the time of transplanting. But, plants that you will be growing directly in the containers will need thinning. The number of seedlings that you thin or the spacing that you will be providing for the plants will rely on whether you want the vegetables to grow full size or you want them to harvest early. For instance, if you want tiny carrots, the seedlings can be spaced tightly. But, if you want large-sized carrots, you will need to provide the seedlings with more space.

Root vegetables might be very sensitive to the process of thinning, as disturbing the young root system can result in deformation.

Mulching

Mulching plays an important part in gardens of all types. You can add a layer of compost under the topsoil for retaining moisture. It can also help in deterring weeds. If the temperature of the soil tends to change drastically, it can be harmful to the plants. So, adding mulch to the soil can also help in regulating the soil temperature to a great extent. You can also use shredded leaves and straws for adding mulch to the soil.

Fertilizing

Just like watering, feeding the plants is also equally important. Plants that are grown using traditional methods in the soil can easily expand their roots for seeking nutrients. But, in the case of container gardening, plants cannot expand their roots outside the containers. So, it can be said that the plants grown in containers will be depending on your for their nourishment. You can use organic fertilizers for container gardening. But, the plants will be exhausting all the available nutrients within a few days. So, you can opt for liquid fertilizers for providing the plants with the required nutrients daily. You can make liquid fertilizer on your own or get some from the market.

You can find various types of liquid fertilizers in the market. You will need to check the N-P-K ratio on the pack. In this ratio, N stands for nitrogen, P stands for phosphorus, and K stands for potassium. You can get the fertilizer that comes with an equal proportion of all the three nutrients. For fruiting plants, you will need to get the fertilizer that comes with a higher value of K. If you are willing to make your own liquid fertilizer, you can get various information from the internet.

Fruiting veggies such as tomatoes will need to be fed weekly. But, make sure that you do not use fertilizer for the seedlings as it can burn out the plants. Generally, you can feed the plants in alternating weeks, maintaining the proportion suggested by the manufacturer.

Harvesting

You can harvest the vegetables either midway or after a full growing cycle. It is always better to harvest during the morning. If you are growing various types of veggies at the same time, you will need to keep track of their harvesting time. Different vegetables come with different periods of harvesting. However, it is better not to keep the vegetables for too long in the garden after the period of harvesting is over. It can result in pest infestation and diseases as well.

Weeding

Weed controlling in container gardening might turn out to be a daunting task. In the traditional gardens where weeding is possible by using sprays, it cannot be done in container gardening. The use of chemicals needs to be limited in container gardening. So, anything that you do regarding weeding needs to be done with your hands. You will need to keep the containers properly sanitized so that weeds cannot produce their seeds. After the harvesting period is over, and the containers are empty, try to chemically control the growth of weeds. You can install fresh stones or weed fabric if required. Herbicides can be used directly on the stones and weed fabric.

Pest Control

Controlling pests is a common problem that is shared by the majority of the gardeners of container gardens. The good aspect of container gardening is that container gardens are more accessible in nature and need frequent watering. You can find out problems before they tend to get out of your hands. Here are some steps that you can follow for effective pest control in container gardens.

- Do not try to reuse the potting mix. Try to avoid reusing the potting soil, specifically if it contained plants that were attacked by pests or diseases. Even when the soil looks okay, it might be contaminated with diseases and pests. Soil mix can also contain larvae or eggs of various insects.
- Try to clean the containers whenever you can. It can help in preventing pests to a great extent. Before planting new plants, scrub the containers with water and detergent. The containers that might have been subjected to diseases and pests need to be soaked in a bleach solution. Rinse the containers properly and permit them to get dried properly under the sun.
- Provide the plants with all that they need. You will need to provide the plants with the perfect combination of fertilizer, water, and sun. When the plants are healthy, they can easily fight against pests. Remove dead leaves and stems that can attract insects and pests.
- Do not try to keep infected plants in the garden. Some pests can spread very rapidly from one plant to the others. So, it is better to remove all those plants that are infected.
- Opt for regular inspection of the garden. If you notice something, take the necessary actions for dealing with the same before it spreads.
- Not all types of insects are harmful to plants. There are certain insects that can eat the harmful ones, for example, ladybugs.

Pros & Cons

There are various reasons that make container gardening a better option than traditional gardening. The primary benefit of container gardening is that you can move the containers wherever you want to. This section is all about the pros and cons of container gardening. Let's have a look at them.

Pros

- Containers improve the overall accessibility. It allows everyone to get indulged in gardening despite the various types of circumstances. You might have physical limitations that prevent you from bending down and gardening. With container gardening, problems of this kind can be solved. You can position the containers anywhere you want that can make working on them an easy job. Containers can make your dream of gardening turn into reality by providing you with the opportunity of decking up your balcony or terrace.

- Were you thinking about planting some vegetables for a long time but getting overwhelmed with the thought of managing them? In that case, container gardening can provide you with the required help. It is much more manageable because of the small size, and thus you can easily build your confidence in gardening. You can control the conditions of growing according to the needs of the plants.

- With the help of container gardening, you can get the chance of showcasing your creativity. Containers are available in shapes and sizes of all types. In fact, anything around you can be reused as a container for your garden when you use a little bit of your imagination, such as extra bathtub, watering cans, boots, and so on. You can create endless possibilities with container gardening with no form of restrictions at all. You can get the chance to decorate your windowsills as well.

Cons

- The containers tend to dry out faster. Although they can be placed anywhere, you will still need to water them frequently. The requirement of water increases during the summer heat when the soil in the container can dry out completely. You might even need to water them two to three times a day.
- You might need to provide the plants with additional feeding when compared to gardening in soil. This is mainly because the space in the containers is limited, and the system of roots cannot expand out for more nutrients from the soil. Even when you have the best medium of growth, supplemental feeding is necessary.
- You won't be able to use soil from the garden for filling the containers. So, you will need to buy soil mix from the market that is not cheap. The type of soil that you will need will depend on the type of plants that you are growing. So, if you are growing plants of various types at once, you will need to get the soil of different compositions.
- Plants can outgrow the containers. So, you will need to replace the small containers with large ones as the plants tend to grow bigger in size.

CHAPTER 3

In-Ground Gardening

There is something special about in-ground gardening that can easily announce to the world about your seriousness towards the pursuits of gardening. Maybe it is because this method has been nurtured for several years. Or, it is because the vegetables and fruits seem like they just sprung from Mother Nature. In-ground gardening is the most basic type of gardening that involves growing plants in your backyard or garden. It is simple in nature when compared to the other sectors of gardening and provides plenty of food when done right. It uses the soil that is available in the garden and thus can be regarded as an inexpensive way of growing crops on your own.

Well, as you decide to grow vegetables in your garden, you can enjoy several benefits. You will be able to make use of the area that is available to you without a problem of any kind. The best part is that there is no need to get soil from the outside if the soil in your garden is fine for growing plants. The majority of soils are perfect for gardening, provided that the soil is mulched, watered, and tilted. You can grow vegetables in your garden even without the use of any kind of amendments if the soil is fine for plant growth. You will be able to grow a plentiful harvest without any worries.

The work involved in starting up your garden is quite less. A flat area with proper drainage can be used for growing plants. You have the option of growing various types of crops at one time, without thinking about nutrients. This is because the root systems of plants can easily expand in the soil for getting extra water and nutrients. Also, the in-ground gardens tend to dry out less, and thus the requirement of water is also less. You can replace the garden with a crop of another type whenever you want.

You will not need to think about the shape of the garden, and you can make use of all the space that you have got. You can take advantage of the flat surface and will make the whole task of gardening a lot easier for you. However, if the soil in your garden is not that great, there is something that you can do. You will need to replace that with certain microbial agents that will help in regenerating the quality of the soil. If you want to grow large-scale crops at one time, in-ground gardening is the perfect choice for you. But, keeping away pests and diseases from the growing plants might turn out to be a challenge for you. As plants will be close to the ground, the infestation of pests will be more. You can add insecticides and pesticides to the plants, but it can degrade the soil quality to a great extent.

You can develop a checklist for all the required components such as water, sunlight, nutrients, and so on. It will make your task of gardening much easier. Let us start with the basics of in-gardening first, and then we will slowly progress to the other components of the same.

Basics

In-ground gardening will also need some of the basic components for growing plants such as water, nutrients, drainage, sunlight, and so on. For getting the most out of your garden, you will need to make sure that plants are getting all that they need in proper quantities.

Sun

The majority of the plants need about 6 – 8 hours of full sunlight per day. So, you will need to set up the garden in such a spot where sunlight is available readily all throughout the day. You will need to observe your garden to find out which place receives the best sunlight with no shade. In case your garden is under shade the majority of the time, there is nothing to worry about. You won't be able to grow vegetables like tomatoes in the shade, but the cultivation of other veggies and fruits is possible. Never try to omit the step of proper sunlight as plants won't be able to thrive without light. So, when you choose the spot, choose it wisely. You will need to arrange the plants in the way of making the best use of light and space. You can group the tall vegetables on the northern side of your garden. This will make sure that the tall plants won't shade the shorter ones.

It is always better to grow small and fast-maturing vegetables between the large plants. In case the temperature rises a lot, you will need to protect the plants from excess heat. Sunlight is necessary for plant growth, but an excess of it can dry out plants.

Drainage

The drainage system can actually create havoc for your vegetable garden, specifically after a period of heavy rain. When the drainage of your garden is poor, the logged water can prevent oxygen from reaching the roots and thus will result in dying plants. Also, when you have logged water near the root area, it can lead to root rot. It can give rise to fungus and pest infestation as well—the majority of the drainage problems of in-ground gardening results from clayey soil. Clay soil is denser than loamy or sandy soil. So, it allows the rainwater to filter out very slowly. Not only rainwater, but normal garden watering also needs proper drainage.

To prevent problems of drainage, make sure that the area of gardening is higher than the surrounding areas. In case the spot of gardening is lower than the surrounding area, water will get logged easily. You can also create an underground drain for an effective solution of drainage. The most widely used type of underground drain is the French drain. You will need to make a ditch all around the garden filled with gravel. You can create a small drainage system for redirecting water out of the garden bed. Maintaining drainage for in-ground gardens might turn out to be a tough job.

Water

Watering the plants will be of no value if the water tends to run down the area of the root system. This is most likely to happen when you water the plants quickly or supply too much water at a time. Watering is most effective when done slowly. When it comes to the watering of an in-ground garden, there is no definite rule. It will depend completely on the idea and knowledge of the gardener. It is a kind of judgment that will rely on various things such as soil, plant type, time, weather, and several other variables. As you build up a garden on your own, you will get an idea about the needs of the plants. You can get proper knowledge first about the various types of plants before planting them in your garden. This will help you to determine the water requirement for the plants.

No matter how much you water or how often you water, make sure that you do it in the morning. This helps in proper absorption of water by the plant roots while the excess water gets dried off by the day heat. Also, it can prevent the plants from various types of diseases and pests. For in-ground gardens, you can use an automatic timer for watering the plants along with a sprinkler. This can ease up your job a lot. You will just need to ensure the weather and adjust the frequency of watering according to that. During the hot summer days, you might even need to water the plants two to three times a day. You can also use mulch to prevent water runoffs. In case the plants need precise watering, you can opt for a drip system. It will help in providing the plants with the required amount of water.

In case the garden soil is heavy in nature, water might take a long time to get to the plant roots. So, make sure you water the plants slowly and allow the plants a long drink.

Tip: Try to use a shovel for checking the progress of water up to the root system.

Logistics

Make sure that you establish the garden in a place that is free from pests and diseases. While setting up the garden, you will need to leave some space all around the garden for proper accessibility from all sides. In case you are growing plants in rows, you can leave a wide space between the rows that will make the task of planting, weeding, watering, and others easier for you. Do not make the garden too constrained, otherwise it will be turn out to be tough for you to manage the garden.

If you want to set up a large garden, try to set it up close to the water source. Make sure that all the tools and equipment are handy in your garden. You will need to leave some space for transportation, for example, a wheelbarrow. Try to set up the garden away from large trees as it can shade the garden.

Size

In case you are confused about the size of your vegetable garden, there is no definite size for it. According to some gardeners, having a garden of 100 sq. Ft. is a perfect size, while for some, it is 150 sq. Ft. All these 'perfect' sizings cannot be correct as different families come with different needs. Also, the plants will vary in size. So, the size of the garden will depend on the type of vegetables that you want to grow.

You can find out the size of your garden by determining the purpose of your garden first. Do you want to set up the garden for your kitchen supplies, or do you want to depend on the garden for everything? This is the basic thing that you will need to determine. People set up their garden for various reasons; some want a garden for their hobby while some want to grow some large-size produce. Also, the number of heads that you are trying to feed will affect the garden size. Obviously, if you are the only person who will feed on the garden produce, the size of the garden is not required to be huge. If your family has four members, you will need a garden that is smaller than a family of six and vice versa. It might be a bit tough to assume all these in the first if you are only a beginner in gardening.

If you are opting for succession planting, the size of the garden can be small. For example, if you are willing to grow beans and peas in the same garden, peas can be grown in February, and beans can be grown after that. There are several other plant combinations that are good for the garden. It will be discussed in the upcoming sections. Many people opt for several garden beds at one time. In this, you will need to divide the total garden into several sub-parts. This has nothing to do with the garden size directly but is essential while planning the size of your garden.

The number of times that you will be planting in a year will also determine the size of the garden. You can grow a summer garden with squash, tomatoes, peppers, and cucumbers and then a winter garden with squash, cabbage, and other root vegetables. You can finish off with spring garden of spinach, lettuce, peas, and cabbage. This might seem like more tiring than having one or two gardens per year. But, when done properly, it can help in saving a lot of space. The types of vegetables that you are willing to grow also play an important role. You will need more space for growing tomatoes than carrots or any other root vegetable. Just keep one thing in mind; different plants need a different area for growing. It could actually make more sense to grow small plants with higher yields than growing large vegetables with poor yield.

Building Structures

In-ground does not any kind of structure as such. But, you can make certain structures for providing support to plants of various types. Plants such as peas, beans, and tomatoes might need support when they grow in size. In such cases, you can use a trellis or other supportive structures for the plants.

Before you opt for building a structure for plants, you will need to look after your purpose and budget as well. In case you are looking out for a very basic support system, designing a trellis with sticks and ropes will be fine. But, if you want to create a support system for many plants at one time, you will need a sturdier one. You can also build small fences around the garden to prevent pests and animals from damaging the garden. There are various designs of trellis that you can try out. One such popular design of trellis is the window frame. It is quite easy to build, and you will need a few basic things for building.

Materials Needed for Window Frame Trellis

Old door or window frame

Nails

Hammer

Tape measure

Galvanized wire

Process:

- Place the frame on a surface that is accessible from all sides.
- Start putting nails on the frame at a gap of 6 inches. Use a tape measure for measuring the gap.
- After you are done with putting the nails, now it is time to use the wire for making the mesh.
- Start by placing the wire vertically from one side to the other.
- Now, place the remaining wire horizontally from one side to the other. This way, you will be able to make a cubic wire network on which the plants can take support.
- You can now place the frame where you want to and start planting.

Plants

Growing your own vegetables is always rewarding and fun. But, as you start with it, you will need to begin with a few numbers of plants and good quality of the soil. For being a successful gardener, you will need to understand the requirement of the plants and plan accordingly.

Plant Journal

Keeping a plant journal is very important while growing plants in an in-ground garden. This is because as you will be growing plants over a vast area, it won't be possible for you to maintain them without proper records. It is beneficial when you will be growing plants of various types in your garden. You can maintain a separate journal for each area of the garden bed.

Spacing

The location where you will be setting up the garden is very important. Making the most out of your garden space is much crucial than growing vegetables. Most gardeners dream of having a huge garden of vegetables, a huge site that will be enough for growing anything they want. But, despite that, you will need to maintain the spacing of your garden properly. Whether you want to create a dense vegetable garden or a moderate one without proper spacing, plants cannot grow. This applies especially for in-ground gardens where several plants are grown at one time.

Maintain a space of about 5 – 6 inches between the plants. The best way of maximizing space in your garden is to get rid of rows. Row gardening is suitable for large-scale gardening, but for a home garden, the fewer rows you have, the less space you will need to leave between them. Thus, you will be able to utilize more square feet of the garden while leaving the required space in between.

Companion Planting

Companion planting is important for in-ground gardening. As you grow plants that are compatible with each other, you will be able to control weed, disease, and pests, improve soil quality, and so on. Companions help each other to grow properly and also use the space of the garden efficiently. For example, tall plants can help in providing shade to light-sensitive plants. Vines can help in covering the soil surface while stalks can grow tall.

Roses and Garlic

You can grow rose with garlic as the smell of rose can help in repelling garlic pests. Also, the chives of garlic help in repelling insects that attack rose plants.

Cabbage and Tomato

When you grow tomato and cabbage together, tomato helps in repelling larvae of diamondback moth that feeds on the leaves of cabbage. The moths tend to create large holes on the cabbage leaves that can be prevented by growing tomato plants side by side.

Dill and Cabbage

Cabbage and dill act as a great companion. Dill can be grown with the plants of the cabbage family, such as Brussels sprouts and broccoli. Cabbage helps in providing support to the floppy structure of dills. On the other hand, dills help by attracting useful wasps that can control worms and pests that attack cabbage.

Beans and Corns

Beans help in attracting important insects that can eat away pests of corn like leaf beetles, leafhoppers, and armyworms. The vines of beans can also seek the support of corn stalks.

Spinach and Radish

Planting spinach along with radish can keep away leafminers from the green leaves of radish. Leafminers can also eat away leaves of radish.

Crop Rotation

Crop rotation is an important aspect of in-ground gardening. As you tend to grow crops in the ground, fertility, along with nutrient content of the soil, can get low. Following the system of crop rotation for your garden is a proven way of improving the condition of the garden, without the use of external components.

The main idea behind the concept of crop rotation is to cultivate each group of plants in different parts of the garden every year. The goal is to improve the overall yield along with the health of the plants that you grow in your space. You will need to split the crops into various groups according to their habits and needs. Plants that are of the same type can grow better together. It will be easier for you to provide them with exactly what they need. Also, different crops take different types of nutrients from the soil and are most likely to leave behind certain traces. If you tend to grow the same types of plants every year in the same place, it will be deteriorating the structure and fertility of the soil steadily.

Crop rotation is very effective in dealing with issues of this kind. One of the most basic systems for rotating the crops is by splitting them into four different groups and then plant them in a rotation schedule of four cycles.

Plant Groups for Crop Rotation

The large-scale growers can develop various types of complicated systems that involve green manures, fallow years, and several other considerations that are industry-specific. But, if you are trying to opt for a small home-grown garden and willing to rotate the crops, you can split them into four simple groups.

- **Brassicas:** This group consists of kale, cabbage, Brussels sprouts, broccoli, cauliflower, kale, and other friends of this group. This group of crops is prone to clubroot disease that tends to build up in the soil very quickly when the same crops are grown repeatedly in the same soil.
- **Legumes:** Beans and peas are the most common members of this group. This group of crops helps in fixing nitrogen in the soil. Thus, they can work as a natural fertilizer for all the crops that follow them in the system of crop rotation.
- **Potatoes:** Although potatoes are an underground crop, they are treated as a group of rotation within their own growth. The primary reason behind this is that the harvesting process of potatoes needs excessive digging of the soil. This acts as an important role in the rotation. You can also grow chilies, tomatoes, and peppers within this group as they come with the same kind of requirement.
- **Roots:** This group consists of several plant families. But, each member crop produces an important portion of the crop under the soil. Some of the most common examples are onion, garlic, carrot, beets, and radish.

Crop Rotation and Its Benefits for In-Ground Gardening

Apart from the benefits of crop rotation that you have already learned from the previous chapters, crop rotation comes with other benefits as well.

- As you grow crops of the same group together, they will have similar harvesting and sowing times. So, it will make the process of space management much easier.
- Different groups of plants come with different root system depth. Crop rotation helps in spreading the nutritional load over several layers of the soil year after year. This will provide the layers more time for recovery.
- Similar group of crops can benefit from common mulching, watering, and also feeding regimens.
- Crop rotation also helps in preventing pests that are crop-specific from establishing in the garden.

Planning Crop Rotation

Before you star crop rotation in your garden, it will be better for you to make a working plan first. Start by dividing the garden into four different sections. Make sure that each section has adequate drainage, sunlight, and also protection from wind. You will need to set aside each plot for each of the plant groups for every year of the crop rotating cycle. After that, you will need to move each section of the crop down the other section by following this list.

- Group 1: Legumes

- Group 2: Brassicas
- Group 3: Onions and roots
- Group 4: Potatoes

It is very important to plant the crops in this order. It works the best as in the very first stage, legumes will take nitrogen from the air and will fix the same in the soil. Brassicas will be able to thrive on the extra nitrogen and is the best for following legumes in the rotation cycle. As you plant roots after brassicas, nutrients from the lower part of the soil will be used up while providing the upper level of the soil a chance for recovery. In the last, as you dig up the soil, the soil will get a thorough rejuvenation at the end of the rotation cycle.

You can follow another rotating crop cycle in which the steps are identical, like the previous one.

- Group 1: Legumes – Beans and peas
- Group 2: Leaf crops – Cabbage, spinach, rocket, lettuce, etc.
- Group 3: Root crops – Turnip, onion, radish, carrot, potato, etc.
- Group 4: Fruit crops – Pumpkin, tomato, cucumber, eggplant, capsicum, zucchini, etc.

It is true that crop rotation is not meant for everyone. You will need proper knowledge along with planning for carrying out successful crop rotation. But, if you are willing to use natural and sustainable methods most of the time, crop rotation can act as an effective and essential technique for use.

Soil

Healthy soil can guarantee you with healthy plants and also a healthy garden. When you keep the garden soil in proper shape, you will not need pesticides and fertilizers for the soil. Organic soil comes with a high proportion of humus. Humus is the final result of decaying objects such as grass clippings, leaves, and compost. It can hold water very well but also comes with great drainage qualities. Good garden soil will be fluffy and loose in character. It needs to be filled with air that is needed for the plant roots. It also needs to have enough minerals to assist in the proper growth of plants.

Soil pH

The pH of the soil needs to be neutral for ensuring the proper growth of plants. Having a pH level between 6.0 and 6.8 is taken to be the best. There are certain plants that need acidic soil for growing. But, such plants cannot be included within the group of garden vegetables. Wood ash can be used to raise the level of pH. But, make sure that you do not use an excessive amount of wood ash as it can result in increasing the level of pH excessively. It might also take away nutrients from the soil. So, proper care needs to be taken. You will need to spread a light amount of the same on the topsoil during fall. Ensure that you turn the soil properly during the spring.

Soil Density

Along with the pH of your garden soil, it is also very important to determine the texture and density of the same. The texture and density of the soil will depend on the total amount of silt, sand, and clay that it holds. Sand is composed of the biggest particles of soil and feels gritty when touched. Silt particles tend to be slippery when moist and feel like powder as you dry them. You are not required to be an expert in determining the density and texture of the soil. All that you need to do is to take a small amount of soil in your hand and rub it with your fingers. The soil is sandy in nature if it feels gritty. If it feels powdery, the soil is silty. If the soil tends to feel sticky when moist and harsh when you dry it, the soil is clayey in nature.

The majority of the soil will be somewhere in between. You will need to have a kind of soil that drains well and is not sticky in nature. If the soil is rich in clay, it might turn out to be a problem for drainage and might result in waterlogging.

Mix

As you add compost to the soil, it can improve the soil quality. You can get some organic compost from the market and mix it in the soil before planting the crops. Compost, along with other types of organic matter, helps in holding the soil particles together and retains moisture very well. The soil will be able to reserve the nutrients as well that are made available for the plants. Make sure that you mix the garden soil from the bottom for mixing all the components of the soil properly. If you just try to dig in the topsoil and start planting crops, it will result in poor growth of plants.

You can use mulch like straws, leaves, shredded bark, and so on for covering the soil. It will help in protecting the soil from high heat and also cold. It will also help in dealing with water loss. Mulching is also effective in deterring the growth of weeds.

Maintenance

Maintaining the nutrients and pH of the soil is not enough for the proper growth of plants. You will need to remove debris from the soil so that pests and diseases cannot develop. One of the primary things that you will need to check is the soil after a period of heavy rain. You can also get a pH meter for keeping a check on the level of pH. Make sure that you opt for removing weeds from the garden soil. If not done properly, weeds can easily destroy the entire garden.

Planting

Spacing in in-gardening matters the most as you have less control over the quality of the soil. The space that you will need to maintain will depend on the types of plants that you will be growing. In case you are growing vining types of vegetables in the garden, you will need to prepare trellis or other support systems for the plants as you sow the seeds.
For growing vegetables in the garden, you can sow the seeds directly in the soil without opting for transplants or seedlings. Well, if you want, you can also grow veggies from transplants. But, in most cases, direct sowing of seeds is preferred.

There are various plants that can grow the best when the seeds are sowed directly in the soil. But how to do that? Well, there are two methods that you can use for sowing the seeds directly in the soil: hill method and trough method. The method that you will choose will rely on the seed type that you are sowing. In case you are not sure which method to opt for, check the description on the seed packets.

Hill Method

In this method, you will need to pile the soil into a mound. This will help in heating up the soil quickly. This is beneficial for the small seeds as they need warmth for germinating. You will need to pile the garden soil into a mound that is about 1 – 2 feet in diameter and about 5 inches in height. Use your fingers for poking small holes at a distance of one to two inches apart in the mound top. You will need to plant one seed in each hole. In case you are not sure about the depth of sowing the seeds, check the seed packet.

After you are done with sowing the seeds, water the seeds gently, you will need to thin the seedlings after they germinate.

Trough Method

This is the simplest way of planting seeds in your garden. You will need to use two fingers for digging a shallow trench. Sprinkle the vegetable seeds evenly and lightly along the trench. Apply a thin layer of soil from the top for closing the seed trench that you have dug. Ensure that you check the details on the seed packet for the depth of sowing the seeds. Moisten the topsoil of the trench gently.

In this case, also, you will need to thin the seedlings as they germinate. In case you are unsure about the spacing of the seedlings, you can check the details on the seed packet.

You can directly sow seeds of root vegetables. They cannot be transplanted well as seedlings as it can disturb the root system. Crops that love heat such as pepper, eggplant, and tomato need long seasons for producing. They cannot grow well when sown directly in the soil. It is better to start them as seedlings from indoors and then transplant the same in garden soil. Other heat-loving crops like squash, cucumber, and pumpkin can be sown directly.

Growing and Harvesting

The growing and harvesting of vegetables that are grown in home gardens can be done very easily. You will need to follow certain tips and suggestions for getting the best results.

Watering

For preventing the growing plants from wilting in hot weather, you will need to water the plants properly. But, how often and how much you will need to water? Majority of the plants depend on proper moisture levels. So, even slight drying of the soil and plants can disturb the plant growth.

Watering Less and Thoroughly

You can water the plants three to four times a week when the temperature is moderate. But, when it is extremely hot, you might even need water the plants two to three times every day. But, it is always better to water the plants with plenty of waterless often rather than watering less often. You will need to ensure that the plants you water during the morning or evening only. As you water cool soil in the morning or in the evening, less amount of water will evaporate when compared to watering during the heat of the day.

Keep the Leaves Dry

It is very important to keep the plant leaves absolutely dry. When you water the leaves, it might give rise to diseases. Also, when you water the leaves in the sun, it can result in burn marks. If leaves are left wet overnight, it can attract fungus and pests.

Avoid Waterlogging

Make sure that water does not get logged near the root area as it can make it difficult for the plant roots to breathe properly.

Thinning

Thinning of plants is a necessary practice that needs to be done for allowing the plants with proper room for growing. Thinning provides the plants with all the requirements for proper growth, such as light, moisture, nutrients, and so on. As you thin seedlings, you will also be able to improve the circulation of air near the root area of the plants. It is important to understand the proper time for thinning the seedlings. In case you are late, overdeveloped roots can damage the other seedlings during the process of thinning. Relying on the type of plants that you are growing, you will need to thin the seedlings enough so that each seedling can have two to three inches of space on all sides.

Learning the process of thinning is not that tough. But, not all plants will be able to handle the process of thinning in the same way. For example, plants that come with a fragile system of roots like cucurbits and beans need to be thinned as fast as possible, before the roots get intertwined with each other. The main aim is to pull out the seedlings that you do not want in the garden, leaving back the healthy seedlings. Root crops are slightly sensitive to the process of thinning and needs to be done with extra care.

Mulching

No matter what you grow, you will need to provide mulch to the soil. It can help in improving the drainage system and also helps in dealing with weeds. It is always recommended to mulch in layers.

Fertilizing

The main key to proper fertilizing is timing. You will need to provide fertilizer to the plants and soil, depending on the needs of the same. Fragile young plants such as tomatoes and pepper might it difficult to deal with fertilizer if applied at an early stage. It can burn the root system of the tender plants. Also, as you decide to use fertilizer for the plants, you will need to determine the needs of the plants. Fertilizers come in various compositions of nutrients, and each plant comes with separate requirements of nutrients.

Harvesting

For getting the best taste of the vegetables from the home garden, you will need to harvest at the perfect time. There is no fixed rule for harvesting. For the best texture and flavor, most of the veggies are harvested before their full maturity. Here are some examples of harvesting vegetables.

- Beans: The perfect time for harvesting beans is before the seeds start bulging. You will need to check them regularly as beans take very little time in going from tough to tender.

- Carrots: It is quite tough to find out the perfect time for harvesting carrots. The top part of the carrot can be seen at the line of soil, and the diameter for your preferred variety can also be seen. In the majority of the cases, if the diameter looks fine, the length will be perfect too.
- Corn: Right after 3 – 4 weeks after the formation of the silk, they will start turning brown and dry. This is the time when you will need to check the kernels. If the kernel gives out milk-like substance when pricked with nails, it is time to harvest.
- Lettuce head: You can harvest lettuce heads when the heads feel firm and full. Very hot weather might result in the bolting of the heads.
- Onion: You can harvest onion right after the top part falls over. You will need to dry the onion before storing it.
- Peas: The pea pods need to feel and look full. You can enjoy sweet peas if you can harvest them before getting plump. You can taste peas before harvesting them.

Weeding

Weeding is very important in gardens of all types. You can opt for weeding during the early morning as the dew can help in turning the soil loose. For deterring weeds for a long time, you can turn the soil regularly. If weeds develop, do not waste any time and pull them out as soon as possible. Mulching can help in minimizing the growth of weed. Remove dead stems and leaves from the garden. Do not keep the garden soil too moist as it can promote the growth of weed. Weeds can eat up soil nutrients, and so proper care needs to be taken.

Pest Control

The majority of gardeners face the problem of pest in their vegetable garden, especially before the time of harvesting. But, sometimes, the infestation of pests can rise to an excessive level. The small-sized pests can create a lot more disturbance in the garden than you can actually think of. Till now, the most useful way in which pests can be controlled is by preventing them from entering the garden. Prevention of pests is not that tough if done properly.

- **Encouraging useful insects:** Beneficial insects can help in eating the small pests that mulch on the growing crops. Lacewings, ladybugs, damsel bugs, pirate bugs, and parasitic wasps are some of the beneficial insects. They can help in keeping the number of pests under proper control. For attracting insects of this kind, you will need to supply them with nectar-rich in carbohydrates. The more beneficial insects you can have in the garden, the more you can keep the infestation of pests under control.
- **Choosing garden plants wisely:** There are certain varieties of plants that are more prone to get infested by pests than others. Prevention of pests in the garden is sometimes as easy as opting for the pest-resistant crops. For instance, if squash bugs tend to attack plants of winter squash, royal acorn can be used as the resistant variety.
- **Employing physical barriers:** A very useful way of preventing pests is by using physical barriers in the garden that can keep out pests from the plants. You can cover the plants that are susceptible to pests with the use of row cover. Make sure

that you tuck in the sides of the cover properly for preventing the sneaky pests from getting inside. But, keep in mind that you will need to open the covers when the plants are ready to flower or produce fruits.

- **Intercropping:** You can prevent pests in the garden by improving the diversity of vegetable growth in your garden. As you start inter-planting various vegetable plants with one another and also with flowering herbs, it will become difficult for the pests to locate the host plants. So, instead of just planting one type of crop in the garden, try to grow two to three varieties of vegetables at once. There are pest-repellent varieties as well that you can learn from the companion planting guide in the next chapter. When you inter-plant, the pests will find it difficult to hone on their dinner.

Pros & Cons

In-ground gardens come with a wide array of pros and cons. It provides several benefits over the other sectors of gardening, such as container gardening and others. Let us have a look at them.

Pros

- You can have more control over the quality of the garden soil. You can easily adjust the texture, condition, and quality of the soil that is suitable for growing crops. Soil composition can be adjusted by adding in certain elements that you need for improving the quality of the soil. You can add organic matter for adding texture and nutrients to the soil.

- The plants can establish deep root systems. As the root system becomes large, the plants will turn out to be bigger and tasty. Also, plants can get the required amount of water and nutrients from the soil by extending the system of roots. So, plants will be able to thrive better in in-ground gardens. The moisture retention power of the soil will also be better, and thus the plants will not suffer from lack of water.
- This form of gardening makes the task of applying fertilizer and insecticides a lot easier. You can spray them wherever you need to.
- You can opt for better drainage by digging a trench all around the garden. You can also use artificial drainage systems to ensure proper drainage.
- You can have more control while controlling pests.
- The cost of setting up an in-ground garden is not that much. There is no need for any extra material, which is the case in raised bed gardening. You will be growing plants from the garden soil only. There is no need to get expensive soil from the market. No extra setup other than trellis and support systems is required as the crops are grown without the use of structured frames.

Cons

- This form of gardening needs more skills and knowledge for growing plants. As the area of growing plants is most likely to be larger than the other sectors of gardening, you will need to be more cautious about the growth of the plants.

- In case you opt for transplantation of the crops, the shock of transplantation can delay the time of harvesting.
- You will need to give more attention while watering the plants. This is because, in this sector of gardening, the majority of water can drain off if the water is supplied at high speed.
- As you will be sowing seeds directly in the garden, you will need to give in more time for thinning the seedlings. Also, thinning might turn out to be a tough job as the seeds will be sown directly in the soil.
- It might turn out to be tough for you to start growing the direct-sown vegetables in hot and cold conditions.
- The plants will take more space if sown directly without the use of transplants. Also, space management might turn out to be a tough thing.

CHAPTER 4

Plant Profiles

Plant profiles can help you in making your gardening venture a lot easier. This chapter is all about the plant profile of various garden plants.

Basil

Scientific name: Ocimumbasilicum

Details: Basil can be grown in the garden for creating wraps. Purple-colored basil can help in creating a focal point in the garden.

Family: Lamiaceae

Season Of Growing: Spring and late spring

Zone: Three through ten

Spacing: Twelve to eighteen inches

Seed harvesting: 40 – 90 days

Seed starting (indoor): 7 – 8 weeks before frost

Outdoor planting (earliest): After frost danger. Ground temperature needs to be 65 degrees Fahrenheit.

Watering: One-inch water every week during the cycle of growth.

Starting

Location: Needs to be full sun

Planting: You will need to cover the seeds with one-inch soil if you plant the seeds directly in your garden.

Growing

You cannot allow basil to dry out. Watering daily is the best thing. For creating bushy plants, you will need to pinch off the top parts of the plants as they start flowering.

Harvesting: You can pull off the basil leaves whenever desired.

Problems: In case you have opted for growing basil in a very warm spot, you will need to choose those varieties in which bolting takes place slowly.

Bell Pepper

Scientific name: Capsicum annum

Details: Bell pepper can be used as a crop for rotation. Do not opt for growing bell peppers in the same place where you have grown peppers, tomatoes, or eggplant the previous year.

Family: Solanaceae

Season of growing: It is best suited for warm climates such as early spring or late spring before summer days. It can also be grown in slightly cold climates.

Zone: Three through ten

Spacing: Fifteen to seventeen inches apart

Seed harvesting: Sixty-five to seventy-five days

Seed starting (indoor): Ten weeks before the last frost. In extreme southern regions, you can plant the seeds in the garden soil directly.

Outdoor planting (earliest): During early spring right after the last frost.

Watering: Two to three inches of water every week.

Starting

Location: Conditions of full sun is needed

Planting: Cover the seeds with a thin layer of soil after sowing.

Growing

If excessive nitrogen is provided to the plants, more leaves will be produced than peppers.

Harvesting: It is better to cut the peppers from the stem instead of just pulling the peppers off. Peppers tend to develop more flavors with time.

Problems: Bell peppers are very much prone to aphids. You can use water and natural soap to deal with them. You might also face the problem of blossom end rot. This type of condition typically gets cleared on its own. In such a case, you can cut out the portion that is affected and consume the fresh part. Another problem that comes with bell pepper is the cucumber mosaic virus. You will need to spend some extra time in pulling out the infected plants and then dispose of the same. In case you face the problem of cucumber mosaic virus, try to opt for a different spot for growing the next year.

Cabbage

Scientific name: Brassica oleracea var. capitata

Details: Some types of cabbage can grow flowers. The leaves of cabbage can be eaten. But, in the majority of the cases, the leaves are used for the purpose of garnishing. You can check the packet of seeds for verifying if the leaves are edible.

Family: Brassicaceae

Season of growing: Plant the seeds during early spring or during late fall

Zone: Three through ten

Spacing: Twelve to seventeen inches apart

Seed harvesting: Fifty to sixty days

Seed starting (indoor): Six to sex weeks before the onset of the last frost

Outdoor planting (earliest): During early spring after you can work on the garden

Watering: You will need to keep the plants properly watered during dry conditions

Starting

Location: Conditions of full sun is needed

Planting: Cabbage plants can easily withstand very light frost

Growing

Cabbage plants come with a very shallow system of roots. You will need to take proper care while cultivating or weeding so that you do not damage the root system.

Harvesting: You can harvest cabbage when the top heads feel firm.

Problems: One of the primary problems of cabbage plants is cabbage aphids. You will need to use strong water spray or insecticidal soap for removing them. Cabbage worms are also very common. You can remove them with your hands or use row covers for keeping them away. In the case of clubroot, you will need to remove the infected plant. If cutworms attack the cabbage plants, you can remove them with your hands.

Broccoli

Scientific name: Brassica oleracea var. italic

Details: If you are willing to grow broccoli in a warm climate, opting for the fall planting will be the best for you. This is because broccoli can easily survive in cold weather.

Family: Brassicaceae

Season of growing: You can grow broccoli during fall, spring, and cool weather.

Zone: Three through ten. In case you live in a warmer zone, you will need to use seeds that are tolerant to heat.

Spacing: Eighteen to twenty-five inches in each row at a distance of three feet apart

Seed harvesting: Fifty to sixty days

Seed starting (indoor): Seven to eight weeks before the period of the last frost of spring. You will need to provide the seedlings with light of fifteen to seventeen hours with the help of fluorescent lighting.

Outdoor planting (earliest): You can plant them before two weeks of the last frost of spring. During fall or warm climates, you can do it ninety to a hundred days prior to the first frost.

Watering: You will need to provide the plants with moderate watering. Make sure that you evenly the root part only and not the head.

Starting

Location: You will need to provide conditions of full sun. You can allow some shade, but in that case, the growth will be slow.

Planting: Broccoli can grow the best in temperatures ranging between 65 degrees Fahrenheit and 72 degrees Fahrenheit. You can sow them outdoors when the temperature of the soil is forty degrees Fahrenheit or lower.

Growing

Broccoli plants can deal with frost very well. As the system of roots is shallow, you will need to use mulch for better growth.

Harvesting: In case you see flowers of yellow color, you will need to harvest the heads immediately. You will have to consume them as soon as possible. You can harvest the center part of each plant with the use of shears for encouraging side shoot growth.

Problems: The most common problem is aphids. You will need to use strong water spray for removing them. If needed, use row covers.

Beet

Scientific name: Beta vulgaris

Details: You can consume beet roots and greens. They can be pickled, roasted, boiled, or grilled for consumption. In case you want to freeze them, you can do that as well.

Family: Chenopodiaceae

Season of growing: In case you are living in a warm climate, you can grow beet during late fall or early spring. If you live in a cold climate, you can

Zone: Three through ten

Spacing: Twelve inches apart

Seed harvesting: Forty to sixty days

Seed starting (indoor): Not suggested

Outdoor planting (earliest): During cool weather, in early spring, when you can work on the garden. In areas where there is no risk of frost, you can sow during fall.

Watering: One-inch water every week

Starting

Location: Conditions of full sun is recommended. You can also grow beet in partial shade.

Planting: Beets cannot be grown in soil that is acidic in nature. The preferred pH level is between six and seven.

Growing

When excessive nitrogen is provided, the top part can grow much better in comparison to the roots.

Harvesting: You can harvest the greens when the height is about five inches. The roots can be harvested when they are about three inches in total diameter.

Problems: Leaf miner is a common problem. You will need to destroy all the affected leaves.

Carrot

Scientific name: Daucus carrot

Details: You can plant carrots after certain weeks for a getting continuous harvest.

Family: Apiaceae

Season of growing: You can grow carrots during fall and spring, relying on your location. You will need to check the zones for the proper time.

Zone: Three through ten

Spacing: Three to five inches apart planted in rows that are two feet apart.

Seed harvesting: Sixty to eighty days

Seed starting (indoor): You can plant them in the garden soil directly as it is better not to transplant them.

Outdoor planting (earliest): Right after the danger of frost is cleared. In areas that are free from frost, you can plant them during fall.

Watering: You will need to keep the plants moist but not at all saturated. You can opt for drip irrigation for the best results.

Starting

Location: Full sun is recommended

Planting: You will need to cover the seeds with one-inch soil after sowing. It is better to sow them in deep and loose soil for better growth of the root system.

Growing

You will need to take care of watering and weeding only. You cannot grow carrots in clayey soil.

Harvesting: Just twist the top part and pull out the roots. Make sure that you do not break the top part. Cut the tops for storage.

Problems: One of the most common problems is aster yellow disease. This disease can result in short tops and roots with hair. You can use sticky traps for keeping the pest away from the plants. Another problem is fusarium. It can result in the rotting of roots when the carrots are in the ground right before the time of harvesting.

Cilantro

Scientific name: Coriandrum sativum

Details: You can harvest them as cilantro (fresh herb) or as coriander seed. For getting cilantro, you will need to harvest once the leaves appear right before flowering. For getting coriander, you will need to harvest the seeds after they are grayish-brown in color.

Family: Apiaceae

Season of growing: During early summer and spring

Zone: Three through ten

Spacing: Eleven to fifteen inches

Seed harvesting: Seventy to ninety days

Seed starting (indoor): Seven to eight weeks before the last frost

Outdoor planting (earliest): Right after frost danger

Watering: Cilantro will need one-inch water every week

Starting

Location: Conditions of full sun are recommended

Planting: Cover the seeds with a light layer of soil. You can plant after three weeks continuously for a steady harvest.

Growing

There is no need to provide fertilizer to the plants.

Harvesting: You will need to cut the greens at two inches from the ground.

Problems: The primary problem is wilting. You will need to water the plants properly for preventing this.

Chives

Scientific name: Allium schoenoprasum

Details: They can act as a good focal point in the garden and can also be used for various cuisines.

Family: Amaryllidaceae

Season of growing: During late spring

Zone: Three through ten

Spacing: Four to five inches apart

Seed harvesting: Eighty to ninety days

Seed starting (indoor): Nine to ten weeks before the last frost of spring

Outdoor planting (earliest): After the heavy frosting danger

Watering: You will need to water the seedlings properly right after planting. The plants will need one inch of water every week.

Starting

Location: Conditions of full sun is required

Planting: The seeds need to be covered with half-inch soil

Growing

The only maintenance that is required is watering and weeding.

Harvesting: You will need to clip the plants one inch above the level of the ground. The top portion will regrow.

Problems: There is no problem as such.

Corn

Scientific name: Zea mays

Details: You will need to keep the various varieties away from each other for preventing cross-pollination. It can also affect the quality and flavor of the corn after harvesting.

Family: Poaceae

Season of growing: During late spring

Zone: Three through ten

Spacing: Five to seven inches in straight rows at three inches apart

Seed harvesting: Eighty to ninety days

Seed starting (indoor): You can sow them directly in the garden soil.

Outdoor planting (earliest): Right after frost

Watering: The plants will need one to two inches of water every week during the cycle of growth. You can opt for drip or hose irrigation for the best results.

Starting

Location: Condition of full sun is needed for proper growth.

Planting: You will need to cover the seeds with a soil layer of one inch after sowing. Mix fertilizer of slow-releasing character in the soil before planting. You can follow the directions on the label for proper usage and mixing.

Growing

The only required maintenance is watering and weeding.

Harvesting: Each stalk of corn plant can produce two corn ears. But, if you for the hybrid varieties, you can get more yield. The perfect time of harvesting is when the silk ends of the ears dry out and are brown in color. You can pinch your nails in corn kernels for checking whether they are firm or not. You might even need to pull out the corn husk a bit for checking the condition of the produce. Give a small twist to the corn ear, and a firm tug is enough for releasing the same.

Problems: The primary problem of corn is corn earworm. Such pests can be found at the end part of the corn ears. You will need to trim and remove the corn ends. You can also use mineral oil of food-grade quality in the corn ear ends as the silk changes its color to brown. Mild insecticide can be used for dealing with pests as well.

Onion

Scientific name: Allium cepa

Details: You can harvest onions in the form of green onion or as onion bulbs when full maturity is allowed.

Family: Amaryllidaceae

Season of growing: Depending on the growing location, onion can be grown in spring and during fall. You can check the zones for the proper time.

Zones: Three through ten

Spacing: Three to five inches apart in straight rows that are one feet part

Seed harvesting: If you are planting seeds, it will take 120 to 140 days. If you are planting for green onion, it will take 70 to 100 days. For getting onion bulbs, it will take 90 to 120 days.

Seed starting (indoor): Seven to ten weeks prior to the last frost of spring

Outdoor planting (earliest): After the danger of frost

Watering: You will need to keep the root area and the tops dry. Watering the plants with drip or ditch irrigation is recommended.

Starting

Location: Conditions of full sun is needed

Planting: You will need to plant the sets of onion by covering the white part. Cover the seeds with half-inch soil after sowing.

Growing

As onions come with a shallow system of roots, you will need to provide them with enough water most of the time. Try not to make the top part wet.

Harvesting: You can harvest bulbs of onion as the tops start turning yellow in color. Bend the tops and pull out the bulbs.

Problems: Onions are not much prone to pests.

Gardening Resources

- American Hemerocallis Society: www.daylillies.org
- United States Department Of Agriculture: www.usda.gov.in
- American Hosta Society: www.americanhostasociety.org
- Perennial Plant Association: www.perennialplant.org
- Royal Horticultural Society: www.rhs.org.uk

CHAPTER 5

List Of Common Gardening Terms

There are certain gardening terms that you will need to know before you opt for the world of gardening. Let's have a look at them.

- **Annuals:** Variety of plants that tend to complete their cycle of life within one year or even less than that. Annual varieties of crops can produce profusely for a long period.

- **Biennials:** Both vegetables and flowers that tend to complete their cycle of life within two years. They tend to show the growth of leaves in the first year and produce fruits and flowers in the next.
- **Baby greens:** Leafy herbs and green veggies that are harvested when they are 2 – 4 inches tall.
- **Bolting:** The condition of early flowering in edible type crops that result in non-tasty plants.
- **Burpless cucumbers:** Cucumber variety that does not produce a chemical known as cucurbitacin. This chemical is bitter in taste and can result in slight indigestion.
- **Cold climate:** Freezing temperatures, typically USDA zones ten and even cooler.
- **Companion planting:** Growing different types of plants together that can benefit from each other. For instance, growing plants that can attract pollinators right next to plants that need pollination.
- **Compost:** Organic matter that is made from decomposed materials of plants. It is used for replenishing the nutrients of the soil and for reducing landfill waste.
- **Cover crop:** Plants that can grow fast, such as legumes, grains, or grass, that are used for one or even more than one quality of enhancing the soil quality. Such crops are removed from the garden before they start producing seeds.
- **Crop:** Plants that are grown for harvest, such as vegetables and cutting flowers.
- **Days to emerge:** The total number of days, on average, that will be taken by a seedling for emerging from the soil surface or from the medium under favorable conditions.

- **Days to harvest:** The total number of days from sowing of seeds to harvesting.
- **Deadheading:** Cutting off spent flowers from plants for encouraging blooming again. It is done for extending the period of blooming.
- **Direct sow:** Sowing plant seeds directly in the soil or in the permanent space of growing.
- **Disease resistance:** Exhibiting immunity or less susceptibility against certain diseases in comparison to others.
- **Disease tolerance:** Better ability to thrive with infection stress in comparison to others.
- **Drought tolerance:** Capability of thriving or surviving in conditions of low water. They are also called 'water-wise.'
- **Etiolation:** Having characteristics of weak, lanky, pale growth of plants that results from conditions of low light, or no light.
- **Fairly tolerant to drought:** Capability of surviving or thriving in conditions of low water, but to a fairly less extent than drought-tolerant plants.
- **Frost tolerant crop:** Crops that can tolerate frost and cold weather. The tolerance amount will vary from one plant to the other.
- **Frost sensitive crop:** Crops that cannot tolerate cold weather or frost. Such types of crops can die from freezing temperatures.
- **Fruit:** Capsule of seed that results from flowers, for example, melon and tomato.
- **Full sun:** Having sunlight for six hours or more than that.
- **Germination:** The time when seeds start growing.

- **GMO:** Genetically Modified Organisms. They are engineered genetically, which indicates that the concerned variety has been manipulated at the genetic level in the laboratory.

- **Gynoecious:** Plant that produces flowers for accepting pollens. A plant of pollinator type with flowers that can produce pollen is needed for producing fruits. They can mature very fast and are productive in nature.

- **Hardening off:** The one week to ten days process of acclimatization of plants that started indoors for adapting to outdoor conditions.

- **Heat tolerance:** The capability of resisting issues that are triggered by heat such as bitterness, poor pollination, lacking fruit set, premature flowering, etc.

- **Hybrid:** Two varieties of parent crops are bred for achieving hybrid offspring of the first generation.

- **Indeterminate:** Varieties of tomato that can produce and grow tomatoes all throughout the season until the very first frost.

- **Medium:** Used for the purpose of horticulture, it is the material in which plants are grown.

- **Microgreen:** Leafy, young veggies, and herbs that are usually harvested above the line of soil as the plants develop the cotyledons.

- **Mild climate:** Temperature that is not freezing in nature. USDA zones ten and even warmer can be included in this.

- **Monoecious:** Types of plants that can grow both pollen-receiving and pollen-growing parts.

- **Native:** The plants that originate from a particular zone or place in the world.

- **Organic seed:** Seeds that are grown in organic properties. Guidelines of USDA are followed in regard to the quality of soil, weed control, and pest. Fertilizer uses are also controlled according to the guidelines.
- **Open-pollinated:** Variety of plants that produce seeds that are of true nature, developing into identical types of plants.
- **Part shade/part sun:** Receiving sunlight for a period of 3 – 6 continuously.
- **Perennials:** Types of plants that can live for two years or more than that.
- **Pollination:** Fertilization of flower by insect, wind, birds, etc. The male pollen will reach the female stigma that will produce seeds.
- **Pollinator:** Organism that helps in transferring pollens.
- **Row cover:** Fabric that is used for keeping out pests and also for maintaining the optimal temperature. They are also used for protecting the plants from rain, strong wind, frost, and others.
- **Scarification:** The process in which the outer covering of the seed breaks for permitting moisture inside.
- **Sprout:** Type of germinated seed that is not grown in any kind of medium but is rinsed in plain water several times every day.
- **Thinning:** The process of reducing excess seedlings for providing proper spacing for the plants.
- **Transplanting:** The act of transferring small plants from one place to the other.
- **Vernalization:** Type of cold treatment that helps in inducing flowering in certain varieties.

CHAPTER 6

Companion Planting Guide

Plants require good friends to thrive. Except for the concept of fruiting and growth, plants are idle in nature. Most plants are planted in one spot and do not seem to have any form of control over the environment of growth. But, the relationships between plants are of varied nature, more or less like human relationships. In the communities of plants, there are certain plants that can provide each other with the required support. But, some plants cannot just get along. Just like human beings, plants also compete for space, nutrients, and resources.

Certain types of plants tend to grow rapidly and crowd others. Such plants also take away more of their share of sun, nutrients, and water. Some plants also give out toxins that can disturb the growth of plants and can even kill them. A very common example is the tree of black walnut that produces a toxin named hydrojuglone. Other plants act as the upstanding citizens and help others by providing nutrients to the growing soil and attracting important insects to the plants. They can even help by confusing the other insects that are searching for the host plants.

As an efficient gardener, you will need to be the city planner and mayor of the garden city. When you grow plants with a good set of companions, you can bring prosperity and peace to your town. On the other hand, growing plants of disruptive nature can ruin the garden. As with the planning of your garden city, the manner in which you will be laying out the garden of vegetables is very crucial. Try to avoid as much as you can to plant veggies in huge patches or even long rows. You can opt for interplanting vegetables with herbs and flowers. If you group one type of vegetable in a large area, it can easily attract problematic pests. When you opt for mixing herbs and flowers with the vegetables, pests will find it difficult to find the host plants. The scent of herbs and flowers, and also the color can confuse various pests. Certain herbs and flowers can also attract useful insects to the garden.

The habit of growth is not the only characteristic that you will need to consider while companion planting. You will need to be properly aware of the nutritional requirements of the plants as well. As you grow plants together that need a similar type of nutrients, the plants are most likely to compete for the resources. This can result in slowing the speed of growth of the plants. That is why it is recommended to grow plants that come with comes with complementary needs of nutrients.

Companion planting can very well mimic the characteristics of nature. When you grow crops that can complement each other naturally, several problems related to conventional farming can be avoided with ease. All that you will get is a healthy garden that can provide you with high yields. It will be easier for you to maintain a garden of this kind.

Three Sisters

One of the oldest examples of companion planting is Three Sister Planting. It is the growing trio of beans, winter squash, and corn. These three plants were typically grown together by the communities of Native America because of the complementary nature of the plants. The corn plant can grow tall that can support the climbing beans, and the squash will grow low. It can provide shade to the soil area with the big leaves and can also help in discouraging pests and weeds. The growth of beans can supplement the soil with nitrogen.

Now corn, beans, and squash are not the only group of plants that can establish a relationship of this kind. There are various other combinations. You can combine a wide variation of fast-growing crops with the slow-growing ones, aromatic and edible herbs, nitrogen fixers, and stacking plants. This will help you to easily double the possibility of increasing the annual yield for your garden. As an extra benefit, you can grow a crop of alfalfa, white clover, or other nitrogen fixers during the off-season. In this way, you will be able to restore the essential nutrients in the soil. This can guarantee you more harvesting sessions with more percentage of yields.

Let us have a look at some of the most common combinations of growing plants.

Companion Planting Chart

Plants	Companions	Allies	Enemies
Asparagus	Parsley, basil, tomato	Pot marigold can be used for deterring beetles	
Beet	Cabbage family, bush beans, onion, lettuce	Garlic can help in improving flavor and growth	Beet and pole beans can reduce the growth of each other
Beans	Cabbage family, beet (for bush variety only), celery, carrot, cucumber, eggplant, chard, corn, radish, potato, strawberry	Marigold can keep away Mexican beetles. Rosemary and nasturtium can also help in deterring bean beetles. They can be used for improving flavor and growth	Onion, garlic, and shallot can stunt the overall growth of beans
Carrot	Lettuce, beans, pepper, pea, onion, tomato, radish	Chives can improve flavor and growth. Sage and rosemary can be	Dill will slow down growth.

		used for deterring carrot fly.	
Chard	Cabbage family, beans, onion		
Celery	Cabbage family, beans, tomato	Garlic and chives can deter aphids. Nasturtium can help in deterring aphids and bugs	
Cucumber	Cabbage family, beans, pea, corn, tomato, radish	Marigold can be grown for deterring beetles. Nasturtium can deter bugs, beetles, and aphids. It can also help in improving flavor and growth. Tansy can deter beetles, ants, flying insects, and bugs. Oregano can deal with pests.	Sage is not at all for the health of cucumber plants

Corn	Cucumber, beans, melon, pea, parsley, squash, potato, pumpkin	White geranium and odorless marigold can easily prevent Japanese beetles. Pigweed can raise important nutrients from the layer of subsoil so that they are accessible to the corn plants.	Corn and tomato are prone to the same nature of worms.
Lettuce	Cabbage family, beet, onion, carrot, strawberry, radish	Garlic and chives can deter aphids	
Eggplant	Pepper and beans	Marigold can deter nematodes	
Melon	Pumpkin, squash, corn, radish	Marigold can help in deterring beetles. Oregano can provide protection from general pests.	

		Nasturtium can deter beetles and bugs	
Parsley	Corn, tomato, asparagus		
Onion	Cabbage family, beet, carrot, lettuce, chard, pepper, tomato, strawberry	Summer savory and chamomile can help in improving the flavor and growth. Pigweed can raise important nutrients from the layer of subsoil so that they are accessible to the onion plants.	Growth of beans and pea can be stunted by onion
Pepper	Eggplant, carrot, tomato, onion		
Pea	Carrot, beans, corn, turnip, radish, cucumber	Mint can help in improving the flavor and health. Chives can be	Growth of peas can be stunted by onion and garlic

		helpful for deterring aphids	
Pumpkin	Melon, corn, squash	Marigold can help in deterring beetles. Oregano can provide protection from general pests. Nasturtium can deter beetles and bugs.	
Potato	Cabbage family, beans, corn, pea, eggplant	General protection can be provided to potato by planting horseradish by the corners of a patch of potato. Marigold can help in deterring beetles.	Potato and tomato are prone to be attacked by similar blight.
Tomato	Carrot, asparagus, celery, parsley,	Bee balm, mint, and chives can help in improving	Tomato and corn are prone to the same worms.

	cucumber, pepper, onion	flavor and health. Basil can repel mosquitoes and flies.	Potato and tomato are prone to be attacked by similar blight.

CONCLUSION

Thank you for making it through to the end of *The Beginner's Vegetable Garden 2020*. Let's hope it was informative and was able to provide you with all of the tools you need to achieve your goals, whatever they may be.

Now your job is to plan a proper way of setting up a vegetable garden on your own. With the help of the various types of gardening, setting up a garden is not a tough job today. You can opt for the gardening type by relying on your needs and space. If you are willing to grow something on your own, having a vegetable garden as a beginner will be a great choice. Just concentrate on your goal, and you will be able to adapt to the growing system very easily. Make sure that you opt for companion planting for improving the flavor, growth, and health of the plants. Gardening is not that tough. All that you will need to do is spend some time nurturing the knowledge that you have received from this book and put the same into use.

In case you are not sure about the types of plants that you should plant, you can get help from the companion planting guide. As a beginner, it might feel a bit tough to manage disease and pests in the garden. But, with time and practice, you will soon be the master of your own garden.

Finally, if you found this book useful in any way, a review on Amazon is always appreciated!

www.ingramcontent.com/pod-product-compliance
Lightning Source LLC
Chambersburg PA
CBHW081741100526
44592CB00015B/2252